The
North Wales Pilgrim's Way

Taith Pererin Gogledd Cymru

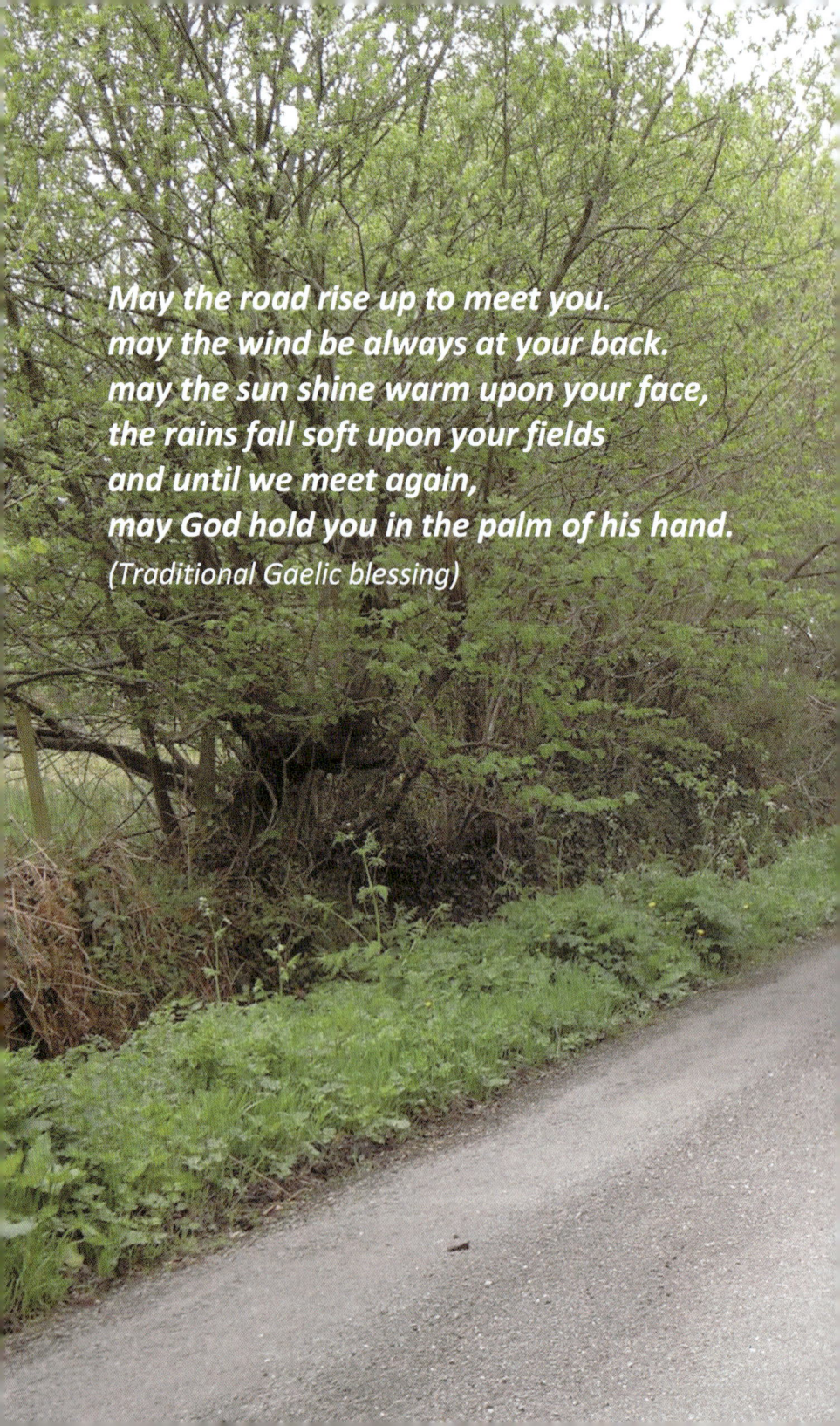

May the road rise up to meet you.
may the wind be always at your back.
may the sun shine warm upon your face,
the rains fall soft upon your fields
and until we meet again,
may God hold you in the palm of his hand.
(Traditional Gaelic blessing)

Patron
Dr. Rowan Williams, The Right Reverend and Right Honourable The Lord Williams of Oystermouth, former Archbishop of Canterbury.

Acknowledgements
Thanks to Ron Williams for originally writing up the route, also to Mike Costello, Nick and Pat Owen, Roger and Meg Mullock, Bryan Monkman, Jenny Potter, Sue and John Last, Janet and Duncan Cameron and Christine Waldron for their contributions to the route descriptions, text, photographs and proof-reading. Route description, layout, design and photography by Chris Potter.

Also, our thanks to the four Local Authorities along the route - Flintshire, Denbighshire, Conwy and Gwynedd – and to representatives of Visit Wales, CADW and the Ramblers Association for their help and assistance in establishing the North Wales Pilgrim's Way. Thanks also to the churches and chapels along the route for their hospitality and encouragement.

Important advice to users of this guide
Whilst we have taken every effort to ensure the accuracy of this guide and that the information within it is correct, neither the author nor the publisher can accept any responsibility for any errors, loss or injury however caused

The quote on the back cover is from Pilgrimages. R.S. Thomas. Between Here and Now. MacMIllan. London. 1981. ©Elodie Thomas 2001

Copyright © 2019 Chris Potter
All rights reserved.
ISBN-9781080333134

CONTENTS

Part one:

Introduction	1
Planning your journey	4
The Saints	7
A guide to Welsh pronunciation	8
Invitation to take the first step	11

Part two: The Route

Basingwerk to Llanasa	12
Llanasa to St Asaph	17
St Asaph to Llansannan	22
Llansannan to Llangernyw	25
Llangernyw to Rowen	31
Rowen to Abergwyngregyn	35
Abergwyngregyn to Bangor	39
Bangor to Llanberis	43
Llanberis to Penygroes	47
Penygroes to Trefor	51
Trefor to Nefyn	55
Nefyn to Tudweiliog	58
Tudweiliog to Aberdaron	60
Your Passport Stamps	64

This guidebook is dedicated to the memory of Meg Mullock,
Howard Holdsworth, Bernice McCabe and Nick Owen
who walked on the inaugural pilgrimage in 2011.

The North Wales Pilgrim's Way was first walked in 2011 by the group of volunteers who had responded to a challenge to re-establish a pilgrimage route across North Wales from Basingwerk Abbey to Bardsey Island. This challenge had been issued by Jenny Potter in January 2010, inspired by the experience of walking the Camino with her husband Chris the previous year. They had started from Le Puy Cathedral in the Auvergne in central France, walking to St. Jean Pied de Port at the foot of the Pyrenees and then on through northern Spain to Santiago de Compostela, taking three months to complete the pilgrimage.

The route in this book has been divided into thirteen sections so that the whole pilgrimage can be completed in two weeks, including spending some hours on Bardsey Island, weather permitting. There are suggestions for accommodation on the website.

This guidebook has been prepared with contributions from many of those first volunteers who have researched the route, walked and re-walked it and written it up. We continue to monitor the path and notify local authorities when issues of maintenance or obstruction occur. The royalties from this book go towards the costs of maintaining the website, the route markers and ongoing publicity.

Centuries ago, pilgrims in their thousands were finding their way to Bardsey Island, Ynys Enlli, drawn there by stories of the special peace to be found at the edge of the western world – drawn to the place of the setting sun, with only the vast ocean between them and the unknown.

Around 1,500 years ago St Cadfan had founded a Christian community there. In the Middle Ages, three pilgrimages to Bardsey were considered the equivalent of one to Rome, and that sense of a sacred place draws pilgrims there still. Pilgrims often carry a scallop shell, originally evidence of having completed the journey to Santiago de Compostella. It became a symbol of pilgrims everywhere - a scoop for water, a receptacle for alms, a sign hung above doors as a mark of welcome.

There is now a route crossing North Wales which has been mapped and waymarked, linking ancient churches dedicated to the saints of the 6th and 7th centuries whose gentle faith, entwined with a sense of the beauty and wonder of nature, still echoes with us today.

Basingwerk Abbey, which served as a hospital to pilgrims going to Holywell in medieval times, marks the start of the Pilgrim's Way. From there the route leads through woodland and over rivers, up mountains and along coast paths, through wilderness and into villages. It celebrates the heritage of those Celtic saints whose stories are lost in the mists of time but whose memory reverberates in ancient churches and at holy wells along the way.

The Pilgrim's Way is a walking route of nearly 140 miles. Tiny stone churches nestled into the hills provide shelter and rest along the Way, much as they would have done in the past. Now the tradition of pilgrimage is being rediscovered and reinvented for a new age. Present day pilgrims have described the experience as "resetting the defaults," as "time out" and "a time to wander and wonder."

A pilgrimage is a walk with an extra dimension. Engaging with the challenges of the terrain and the weather, everyday preoccupations are swept away and the pilgrim is caught up in the bigger picture. Perspectives change, priorities are reassessed.

Crossing the sea in an open boat and finally arriving on Bardsey Island, Ynys Enlli, is the pinnacle of the experience. And carrying home that peace and quietness is the gift that remains.

Planning your Journey

Please check the website for updates www.pilgrims-way-north-wales.org

Backpacking
You should not wild camp without permission. There are facilities for camping along the route.

Travelling Light
The route is reasonably well served by B&Bs, guest houses, hotels and hostels. Individuals and small groups should be able to find suitable accommodation either on the route or just off it. Walking companies suggested on the website will usually, for a charge, pick you up from the route and return you the following morning. You should carry sufficient lunch, snacks and drinks for the day.

You should ensure:
- Your clothing is of good quality. Waterproofs should be carried and worn as necessary. A good pair of boots is essential. The weather can change rapidly in North Wales so be prepared for all eventualities.
- Your rucksack should have a waterproof cover or a liner. Changes of clothing should be carried in stuff bags. These should also be in waterproof bags. A rucksack with a capacity of about 40 litres should be sufficient. Remember the larger the bag, the more you are likely to put into it!

The Countryside Code
Respect Protect Enjoy

Respect other people
- Consider the local community and other people enjoying the outdoors
- Leave gates and property as you find them and follow paths unless wider access is available

Protect the natural environment
- Leave no trace of your visit and take your litter home
- Keep dogs under effective control

Enjoy the outdoors and stay safe
- Plan ahead and be prepared
- Follow advice and local signs

Please note:

- B&Bs, guest houses and hotels will of course provide bedding and towels. Bunkhouses and hostels will normally provide sleeping bags and towels, usually at a charge. Luggage transfer and support is available from our partner providers. (See website).
- Whilst every effort is given to maintaining the waymarks, we recommend that you also take hard copies of the relevant maps with you. The OS Explorer Maps required for the route are: 265, 264 and 254, 253, OL 17.
- The route takes you through remote rural areas with little or no mobile phone signal. Please download any information required for your journey beforehand and save it to your mobile device.
- The North Wales Pilgrim's Way runs through farming regions with footpaths crossing areas where sheep and cattle will be grazing. Dogs must be kept under control.
- Be prepared - suitable footwear and clothing are essential for walking throughout the year. Please carry all the food and drink you need for your journey.
- Toiletries: The "golden rule" is carry only the minimum, a small bar of soap, toothbrush and toothpaste, razor, deodorant, tissues etc. In the summer you will need a high-factor sun cream, insect repellent and a first aid kit. (A small first aid kit in a waterproof cover should always be carried). This should, at an absolute minimum, include painkillers such as paracetamol and ibuprofen; plasters for minor cuts and abrasions; a small selection of sterile dressings for wounds; antiseptic cream, antiseptic wipes, tweezers and scissors and vaseline for blisters.
- Follow the Countryside Code.
- Pilgrim's Passport: Remember to pick up a Pilgrim's Passport if you would like to collect stamps on your journey across the North Wales Pilgrim's Way. Information about where you can get the passport and sites that hold the stamps is available on the website overleaf. There is also space for stamps at the end of this book. You can pick up a Pilgrimage Completion Certificate at the National Trust Centre Porth y Swnt in Aberdaron.

- Bus timetables can be found on the local authority websites: Flintshire CC, Denbighshire CC, Conwy CC and Gwynedd CC and on the Traveline Cymru app.
- Tide tables can be found on the UK Tides app.
- For GPS, you can download the whole route from Viewranger to the app on your phone. The code is NWPW0001.
- Please note that the map drawings in this guide are for reference only and are not to scale.

It can sometimes be difficult to follow the route over open ground, so note that the angle of the arrowhead on the waymark points in the direction you should follow. Route descriptions are believed to be correct at the time of publication. Please note stiles may have been removed and gates inserted without our knowledge so please check the website for any updates or diversions.

For more details see: www.pilgrims-way-north-wales.org

For detailed information on many of the places of interest on the route go to www.historypoints.org and search North Wales Pilgrim's Way. There are QR codes at many of the sites from which you can download the content. It is worth visiting the website before you start. For further information about Bardsey Island and accommodation please see www.bardsey.org.

The Celtic Saints

The period referred to as the dark ages in England is known in Wales as the age of the saints. The sixth, seventh and eight centuries were a time of the flowering of Celtic Christianity in Wales. St. David, the patron saint, was a native of Wales, reputedly the son of St. Non and grandson of Ceredig ap Cunedda, king of Ceredigion. He lived from c.500CE to c.589CE. He was buried at St. David's where his shrine became a place of pilgrimage.

St. Winefride, who lived in the seventh century, was of noble birth. Legend has it that she was courted by Caradog, the son of a local king. She refused his advances and in a fit of anger the prince cut off her head as she tried to reach safety at the church where her uncle, Beuno, was preaching. Her severed head rolled downhill and, at the place where it finally came to rest, a spring issued from the ground. However, that was not the end of Winefride. St Beuno, hearing the clamour outside the church, rushed to the scene and miraculously restored her head to her body, bringing her back to life. St. Winefride's Well commemorates the site where this took place and became known for its healing properties.

Winefride later moved to Gwytherin to an abbey where her aunt was abbess, later succeeding her. She lived there until she died fifteen years later. Her relics were transferred to Shrewsbury Abbey in the twelfth century. There are two churches dedicated to St. Beuno on the Pilgrim's Way: at Clynnog Fawr and, a little further on, at Pistyll on the Lleyn Peninsular.

St. Asaph was the protégé of St. Kentigern (also known as St. Mungo in Scotland). According to legend he carried hot coals in his cloak to warm St. Kentigern who had spent all night praying while standing up to his waist in the River Elwy. He also restored a robin to life. His name is associated not only with St. Asaph cathedral, but also at Llanasa and Pantasaph, both of which are on the Pilgrim's Way.

Other Welsh saints are commemorated along the route: St. Deiniol, who founded the monastery on the site of the present-day Bangor Cathedral; St. Peris and St. Padarn in Llanberis; St. Cwyfan and St. Hywyn in Tudweiliog and Aberdaron and finally St Cadfan, who established St. Mary's Abbey on Bardsey in 516CE.

There are remains of much earlier religious sites high on the moorland above Penmaenmawr which pre-date Christianity by thousands of years. An amazing ring of around thirty stones can still be seen clearly today, and many burial mounds are visible on high ground all along the route.

Wales is a bi-lingual country and, as you travel further west, in many communities Welsh is the natural conversational language and all over Wales public notices are bi-lingual. This basic guide may help you interpret some of the words you come across on your journey. Some words you might hear that are useful ice-breakers: "Diolch", thank you; "bore da", good morning; "noswaith dda", good evening; "nos da", good night.

A guide to pronunciation

A, a	Short, as in cat	C, c	Hard, as in cake
Â, â	Long, as in part	Ch	As in Loch Lomond
E, e	Short, as in get	dd	As 'th' in this or that
Ê, ê	Long, as in café	F, f	As 'v' in voice
I, i	Short, as in dim	Ff, ff	As 'f' in fancy
Î, î	Long, as 'ee' in queen	G, g	Hard as in glove
O, o	Short, as in top	Ng, ng	Soft as in ring
Ô, ô	Long as in tombola	Ll, ll	With tongue in roof of the mouth, blow 'thl'
U, u	Long, as 'ee' in queen	R, r	Trilled, rrrr
W, w	As 'ue' in glue	Rh, rh	Breathy trill, hrrr
Y, y	As 'u' in duck, or 'u' in purse	S, s	As in this
Ŷ, ŷ	Long. As 'ee' in queen	Th, th	As in throw

Some words you might see on notices or maps

Welsh	English	Pronounced
mawr	big	mawer
bach	small	bahch
uchaf	upper	ichav
isaf	lower	issav
afon	river	avon, 'a' as in cap
cwm	valley	koom
bryn	hill	brinn
nant	stream	nant
tŷ	house	tea
hafod	summer farm	havod
felin	mill	vellin
llyn	lake	llin
lôn	road	lorn
pont	bridge	pont
mynydd	mountain	munnith
coed	trees	coyd
merched	ladies	mairched
dynion	men	dunyon

"Pilgrim"

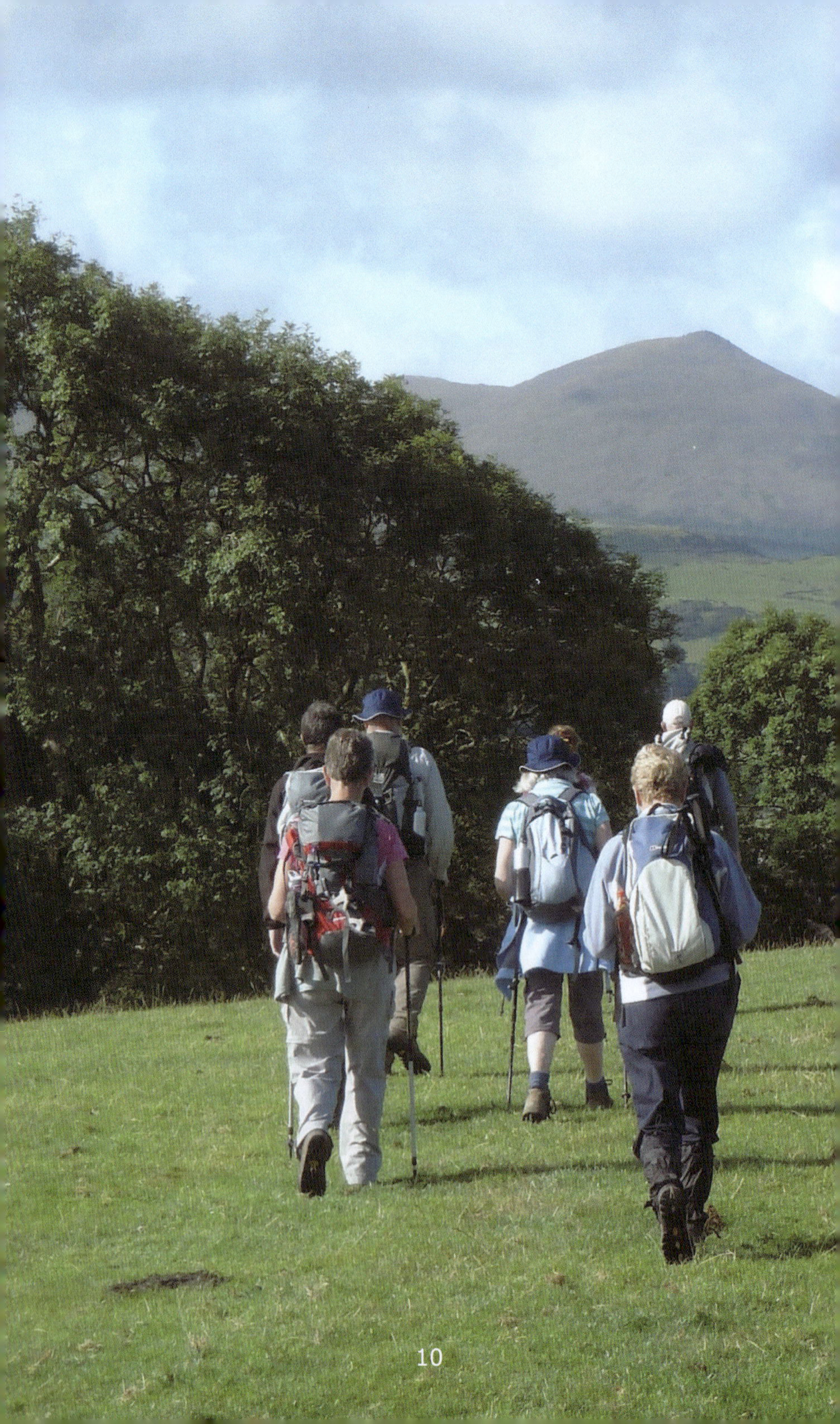

Pilgrims drop everything and set off on a quest. Whether your quest is time out, an escape from routine, pursuit of an interest in ancient history or just to soak yourself in the beauty of the landscape, your footsteps will trace another chapter in the story of pilgrims in North Wales.

Wales is the land of song and poetry and its beauty inspired the saints who established religious enclosures 1,500 years ago along these shores and in remote valleys and hillsides. You will find their names commemorated in churches and holy wells along the route. Ynys Enlli or Bardsey Island was the destination and final resting place for a reputed 20,000 Saints. St Cadfan called it his place of "resurrection".

All these years later, we can still share that sense of Bardsey as a very special place. A deep peace washes over the island. Coloured by sunshine and shadows, with unexpected glimpses and spreading horizons, each journey undertaken has echoes of those that have gone before and each new pilgrimage weaves another thread into that story.

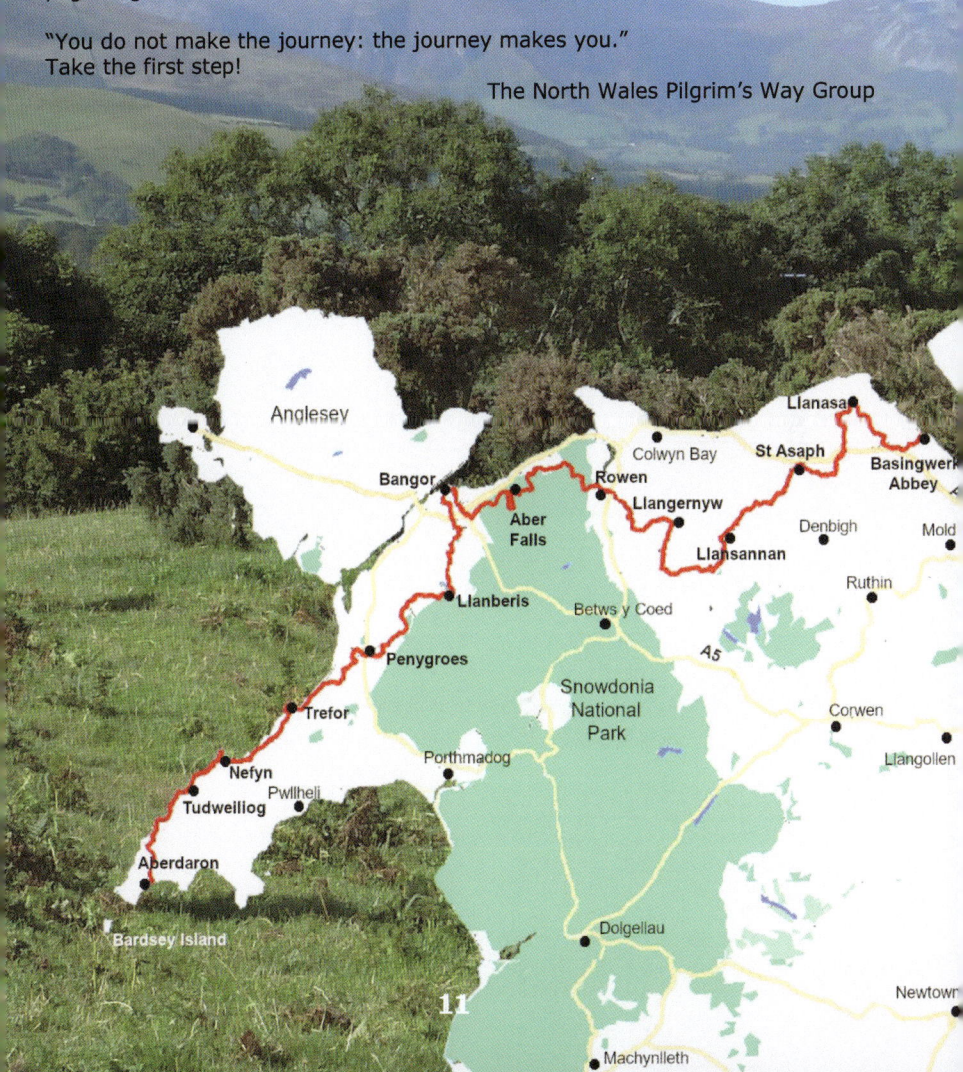

"You do not make the journey: the journey makes you."
Take the first step!

The North Wales Pilgrim's Way Group

Basingwerk to Llanasa

14.2km/8.9 miles
Total Ascent: 478m. **Total Descent:** 361m. **Max. Elevation**: 255m.
Refreshments: Basingwerk, St Winefride's Well, Pantasaph, Llansasa
Toilets: Basingwerk, St Winefride's Well, Pantasaph, Llanasa (pub)
Passport Stamps: Basingwerk, St Winefride's Well, Pantasaph, Whitford, Maen Achwyfan, Llanasa
OS Explorer Map 265

A heritage filled start to the journey from the ruins of the medieval Cistercian Abbey at Basingwerk, up through the remnants of the water powered cotton mills to St. Winefride's Well, one of the seven wonders of Wales. From there a steady climb above Holywell with stunning views of the Dee Estuary and the Lancashire coast. On past the Franciscan Friary at Pantasaph, the 10th Century wheel cross, Maen Achwyfan, through green lanes, pasture and park land to the pretty village of Llanasa.

The mural depicting the North Wales Pilgrim's Way at the start point at Basingwerk was created by unemployed teenagers and supervised by ceramic artist Neil Dalrymple.

You can collect your Pilgrim's Passport from the shop at Greenfield Park or from the shop at St Winefride's Well further up the valley, or you can use the back of this book.

> **Basingwerk Abbey,** originally founded in 1132 by Ranulf II, 4th Earl of Chester, amalgamated with the Cistercian Order in 1147. In the 13th century the abbey found a strong patron in Llewelyn the Great, Prince of Gwynedd, and his son, Dafydd ap Llewelyn, gifted St. Winifride's Well to the abbey. The abbey was disendowed in 1536 under Henry VIII during the Dissolution of the Monasteries. St. Winifride's Well survived, having enjoyed the patronage of Lady Margaret Beaufort, Henry VIII's grandmother.

1. 0.0km/ miles (SH 679 539) Leave the Abbey by walking past the Pilgrim's Way mural towards the Old School and then keep left up the Greenfield Valley. (You may wish to obtain a guide leaflet on the Valley at the Information Office. This tells you about the various sites you will pass on your way.) When you reach the site of the former St Winefride Halt take the footpath (right fork) out of the valley to the main road and to St. Winefride's Well.

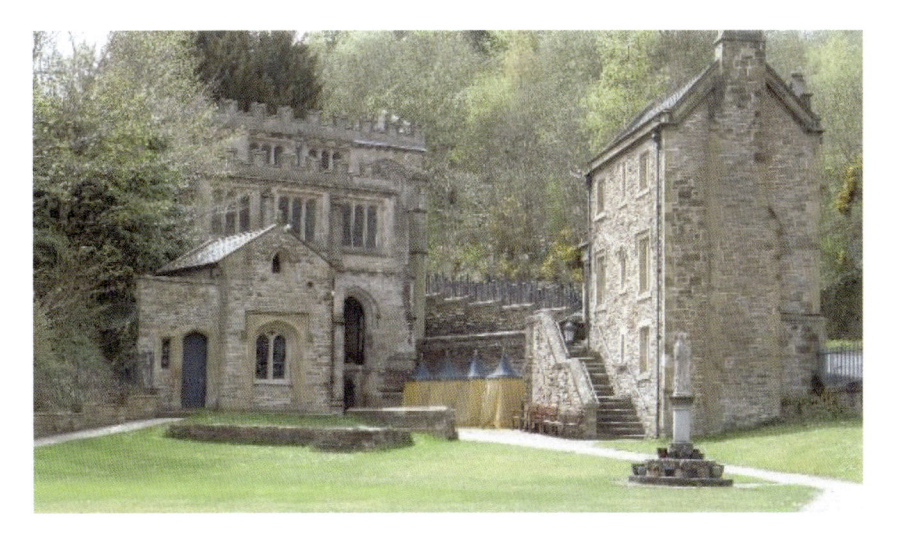

2. 1.4km/0.88 miles (SJ 185 763)

After visiting the Well take the track opposite on the other side of the road past the small car park. The hill to the left of you is the hill where St Beuno performed his miracle. There is a well (unmarked) dedicated to him at this point. Continue up the track until it bends to the right to the farm. At this point go left uphill, crossing over a distinct footpath and continuing towards the houses at the top right-hand corner of the field. Walk past the houses to the road.

3. 2.2km/1.4 miles (SJ 178 763) Taking care, cross the road to go up Brynffynnon Terrace, passing the houses on your left to take the narrow green path on your right. Take this uphill over a stile to go to a gate. Cross the track and go over a stile. Continue uphill with the hedge on your left. Ignore the two stiles going off to the left and go to the stile ahead. Cross over and bear right to walk to the right of the power line (the Pen y Ball trig point is visible on the skyline to your left) to another stile. Cross over and go diagonally left uphill following the power line to a stile in the top corner of the field.

4. 3.1km/1.9 miles
(SJ 172 757)
Cross over this and walk with the fence on your left to a gate/stile. Go through or over and head slightly left to follow the path through the gorse until eventually meeting the fence again on your right. The path goes over the top of the hill, a magnificent viewpoint. Go diagonally down to the left-hand side of the cottage. Cross over the stile, cross the track and another stile and turn right uphill. Go through the gate and bear left to go above the disused quarry. Head directly for the stile and gate ahead. Go through the gate or over the stile and then directly ahead. At the wall around the wood, turn left downhill to a kissing gate.

5. 4.5km/2.8 miles (SJ 162 760) Go through the kissing gate and then over a stone stile on your right into the Churchyard of Pantasaph Friary. Leave the Priory by walking along the path past the entrance to the Stages of the Cross and turn left. At the road junction, turn right to go the next road junction. Cross over the road to the footpath at a stile and gate. Take this path with the hedge on your right to the community of Lloc. Cross over the road and on to the crossroads at the former Rock Inn, go directly across, turn right alongside the road and take the second footpath to the left.

Pantasaph: The Franciscan retreat centre was gifted to the Friars Minor Capuchin of Great Britain as their mother house in 1852. On the thickly wooded hill behind the Friary a path winds up through the Stations of the Cross to a large Calvary sculpture at the summit. The National Padre Pio Centre is located in the Friary gardens.

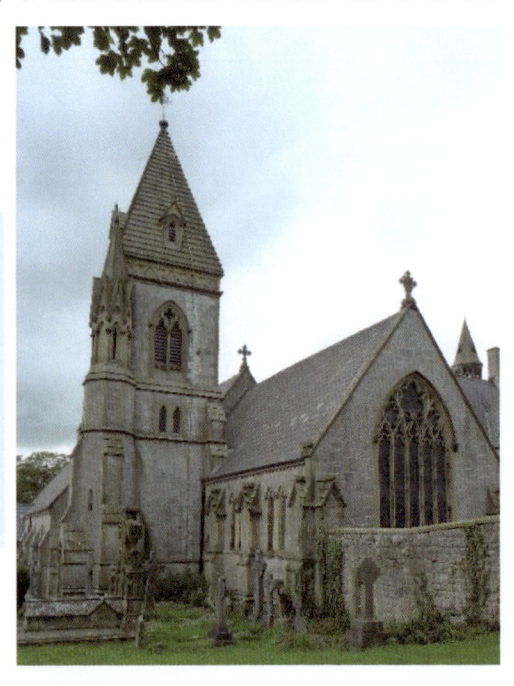

6. 6.72km/4.2 miles
(SJ 145 767) Immediately after passing the house to your right take the track on the right through the woods. At a fork in the path keep right. On leaving the wood turn left onto the footpath and, keeping straight on, in about 900m cross a road on to a bridleway. Immediately go left over a stile and head for the gate to the left of the farmhouse (Garreg Farm). Go through and walk along the bridleway to the right of the farm buildings and up to a track. Turn left along this and shortly turn sharp right to go up hill into the woods (Coed y Garreg). As you enter the woods turn left along the woodland path. Follow this to the stile at the end of the path. To your right is the summit of the hill with its reputed Roman Pharos or beacon, a good place for lunch.

7. 9.2km/ 5.8 miles (SJ 132 782) Return to cross over the stile and go diagonally right to another stile and then to a stone stile alongside the cottage. Turn left to the staggered junction at Penrallt with the late 10th century wheel cross Maen Achwyfan, the tallest in Wales, in the corner of the field. After visiting this mysterious stone, return to the road and turn right and then take the left-hand fork. Pass the small building on your left to a bridleway on the left which passes the cottage (Pen Rallt Farm). Follow this until it becomes a path, passing private woodland and old mine shafts on your right. At the junction continue ahead through two gates and then across two fields with stiles. After the second stile into the edge of woodland turn left, continuing for 300 metres to the gate. Go through the gate and take the waymarked path to the left. Follow this (note the view of Point of Ayr lighthouse) over another two stiles to enter the twin villages of Berthengam and Trelogan.

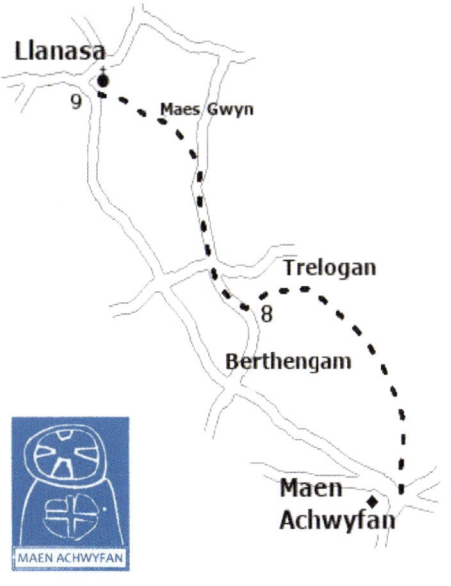

15

8. 12.0km/7.5 miles (SJ 118 799) Turn right at the road (passing a letter box) to the crossroads and Afon Goch pub. Continue down the road ahead for about 0.8km/ 0.5 miles then walk along the drive, left, towards the Pet Rescue Centre at Maes Gwyn. Before you reach the buildings go right over a stile*. Follow the path with the hedge on your left through a gate (stile alongside) and head across the field to walk with the hedge now on your right-hand side. Go over the stile and directly ahead over another two stiles to enter a meadow with parkland trees and Llanasa Village ahead. Walk to the Church of Saints Asaph and Cyndeyrn.

*This footpath can be extremely muddy. To avoid, go over stile on left, passing the Animal Rescue Centre on your right. Cross over a stile and walk with the hedge on your left to another stile. Go over this and the next one to walk up to the road. Turn right along it and follow to the village Llanasa.

Llanasa to St Asaph

18.8km/11.75 miles
Total Ascent: 369m. **Total Descent**: 462m. **Max. Elevation:** 263m.
Refreshments: Llansasa (pub), Trelawnyd (pub), Tremeirchion (pub), St Asaph
Toilets: Llanasa (pub), Trelawnyd (pub), St Asaph
Passport Stamps: Llanasa Church, Trelawnyd Church, Tremeirchion Church, St Asaph Cathedral, St Asaph Parish Church
OS Explorer Map 264

A day spent meandering through fields and country lanes via the Neolithic mound Y Gop above Trelawnyd, a surprising dinosaur or two, enjoying a packed lunch on a hill above St Beuno's with views across the Vale of Clwyd to Snowdonia and on through the village of Tremeirchion to the Cathedral at St Asaph.

1. 0.0km/ miles (SJ 105 814) Leave the village by continuing ahead, passing below the Red Lion pub on right and a house with a pond on left. At the end house turn left to go over the stone stile (or through the gate alongside). Follow a fenced path around and between the buildings and then over the stile. Continue up the field over the stile near a gate and then over another stile alongside a gate. Go straight across the field to the farm gate (to the left of the hedge and a large thatched house) and on to the road.

2. 1.1km/0.7 miles (SJ 104 806) Turn right uphill, passing a post box, and, almost immediately, turn left up a track (signposted Byway /Cilffordd). Follow this to the end and straight on along the farm track towards Tyddyn Uchaf Farm. Go over the stone stile to walk with the hedge on your left to go over another stile. Cross this field diagonally right to go to the lane and turn left along it. Follow the lane over the crossroads towards the wooded hill ahead.

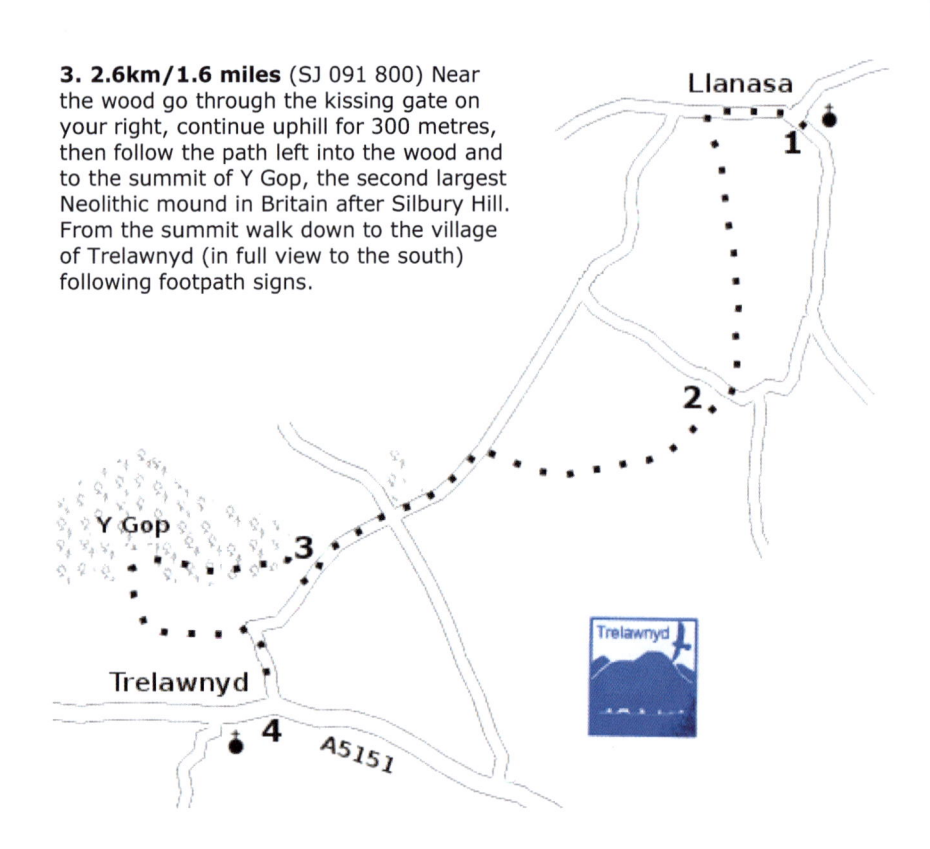

3. 2.6km/1.6 miles (SJ 091 800) Near the wood go through the kissing gate on your right, continue uphill for 300 metres, then follow the path left into the wood and to the summit of Y Gop, the second largest Neolithic mound in Britain after Silbury Hill. From the summit walk down to the village of Trelawnyd (in full view to the south) following footpath signs.

4. 3.9km/2.4 miles (SJ 089 797) From the village use the pedestrian crossing to go to St Michael's Church where you can see the medieval stone preaching cross standing in the churchyard. You will see a similar one in the churchyard at Tremeirchion. Follow the lane past the church to a bridge. After crossing the bridge take the track on your left. Follow this path, passing on your left the entrance to a bungalow (Swyn y Mynydd), to a stile. Cross over on to a bridleway and bear right to take the path ahead to go over a footbridge (farmer's vehicle bridge) into another field. Here head for the top left corner of the field to a stile behind some bushes. Cross over this stile and walk with the hedge on your left to go over another stile to a track. Turn right along this track to a concrete road and pond.

5. 5.7km/3.6 miles (SJ 097 786) Turn right again along the track over the bridge to go either over the stile or through the gate into the field. Continue with the hedge on your left. After two more stiles you reach another stile which takes you left into the wood. Follow the waymarked path over a wooden walkway through the wood and then across a field to a stile. Turn left through another field keeping the hedge on your left to cross another stile to a lane. Turn right and then immediately left over another stile. Go through this field and the next one with the hedge on your right. Cross over the lane and follow the waymarked path as it crosses over four more fields to a track. Keep left ahead and in 100m take the stile left into a field. Cross the corner of the field to another stile onto the lane at Tynewydd. Turn left along this road towards the modern bridge crossing over the A55.

6. 8.6km/5.4 miles (SJ 094 759) Once over the bridge turn left on to the bridleway alongside the A55. Take the stile and waymarked footpath on the right passing directly across the field (due south, passing the tallest of the oak trees), cross a stile to follow a fenced path round the airfield to reach the drive of the farm (Bryn Gwyn Bach) and turn right along it to the gate. At the lane turn right and walk to the crossroads where you turn left uphill to pass a house (Bryntirion).

7. 10.8km/6.75 miles (SJ 089 749) As you reach the brow of the hill take the access track on your right. At the end (by the gate to Penymynydd) go through the kissing gate on your left and walk up to a second kissing gate on your right. Cross the field to the top of the hill (from here there is a very fine view of the Vale of Clwyd with Denbigh to the left, St Asaph ahead and the River Clwyd flowing to the sea at Rhyl to the right). Take the stile on your left (over the wire fence) and follow the footpath diagonally right down the side of the hill to a bridleway. Turn left along this bridleway (part of the Offa's Dyke Path), passing above St Beuno's College.

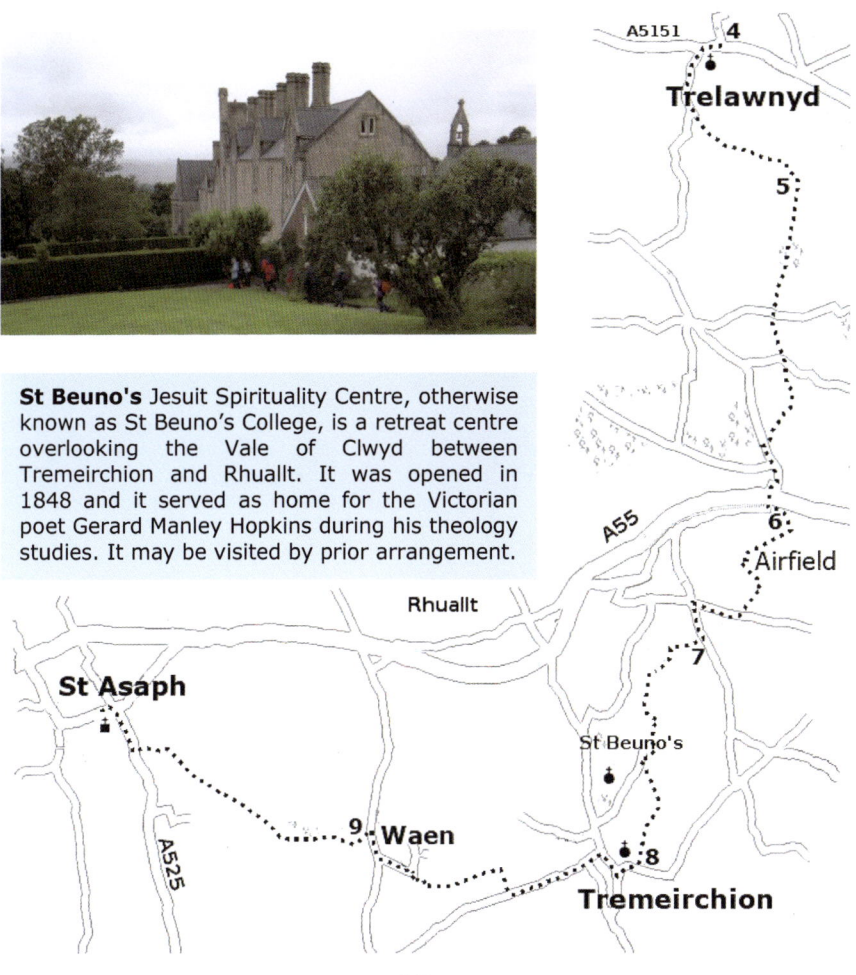

St Beuno's Jesuit Spirituality Centre, otherwise known as St Beuno's College, is a retreat centre overlooking the Vale of Clwyd between Tremeirchion and Rhuallt. It was opened in 1848 and it served as home for the Victorian poet Gerard Manley Hopkins during his theology studies. It may be visited by prior arrangement.

Leave this National Trail after about 200 metres (when it goes uphill) and take the bridleway, right, down towards the village of Tremeirchion. The bridleway becomes a lane and, at the first cottage (Ysgubor) take the footpath over the stile on your left to ford a small stream. Follow this footpath over five fields and stiles to the village of Tremeirchion seen ahead. Turn right to the Church of Corpus Christi.

8. 13.2km/8.25 miles (SJ 083 730) Follow the road downhill from the Church and take the first road to the left - signed Trefnant. Take care walking alongside what can be a very busy road. Follow to the first footpath opposite the entrance to Hafod y Coed to go along a track on your right. Follow this footpath around Plas Coch. After passing the back of the farmhouse go through a gateway on the left and follow the path along the left-hand edge of the field (with the pylons to your right) to a stile in the corner. Cross over and walk down to the lane. Turn left along it to cross a bridge and follow the lane, keeping left, to a T-junction with a Chapel opposite. Turn right to pass the Farmers Arms at Waen.

9. 16.1km/10 miles (SJ 061 733) After passing the pub take the lane on the left. When the lane bends left to a cattle grid, go over the stile on your right. Follow the footpath signs across open fields (view of St. Asaph Cathedral tower). When you reach the bottom of the valley bear right to cross a steel footbridge over the River Clwyd. Follow the waymarked footpath through six fields until you come to a kissing gate in a hedge to join the disused railway track. Turn right. The path leaves the track to pass the school to reach the main road. Turn right to the Cathedral.

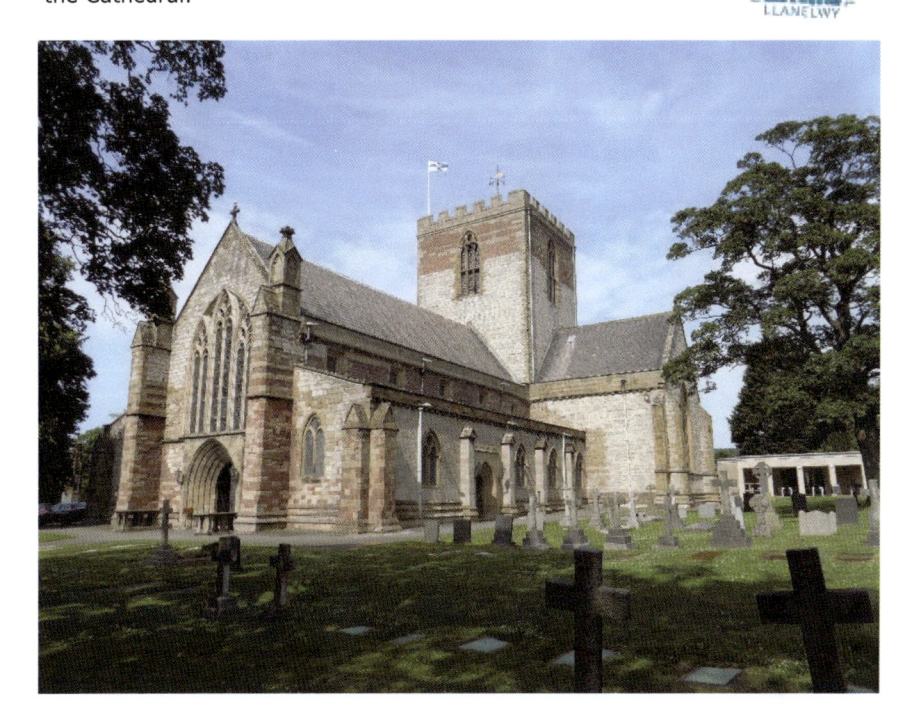

St Asaph Cathedral (Welsh: Eglwys Gadeiriol Llanelwy) is the episcopal seat of the Bishop of St Asaph. The cathedral was established some 1,400 years ago, although the present building dates from the 13th century. It is claimed to be the smallest Anglican cathedral in Great Britain. It houses a copy of the first Welsh translation of the Bible and a monument outside the Cathedral commemorates the translators. A church was originally built on or near the site by Saint Kentigern in the 6th century. Saint Asa (or Asaph), succeeded him as bishop. The earliest parts of the present structure date from the 13th century when a new building was begun on the site after the original stone cathedral was burnt by King Edward I in 1282. The rebellion of Owain Glyndŵr resulted in part of the cathedral being reduced to a ruin for seventy years. The present building was largely built in the reign of Henry Tudor and greatly restored in the 19th century.

St Asaph to Llansannan

17.1km/10.7 miles
Total Ascent: 725m. **Total Descent:** 581m. **Max. Elevation:** 292m.
Refreshments: St Asaph, Llannefydd, Llansannan
Toilets: St Asaph, Llannefydd, Llansannan
Passport Stamps: St Asaph Cathedral, St Asaph Parish Church, Cefn Church, Llannefydd Church and Llansannan Church
OS Explorer Map 264

A pleasant pastoral walk alongside streams and through woodland, crossing rolling countryside and several little bridges to bring you to Llansannan with its church, pub and shops.

1. 0.0km/ miles
(SJ 039 743)
Leave the Cathedral and walk down the High Street and over the bridge. Turn left and continue along this road. Go ahead at the mini roundabout to pass the factory on your left. Take the first road on your left and follow this for 2.6 kms /1.6 miles. Go right when the road forks and you will shortly reach the imposing church at Cefn Meriadog. Go left at the next fork and down to the T-junction. Turn left to Bont Newydd. Cross over the bridge and turn right uphill.

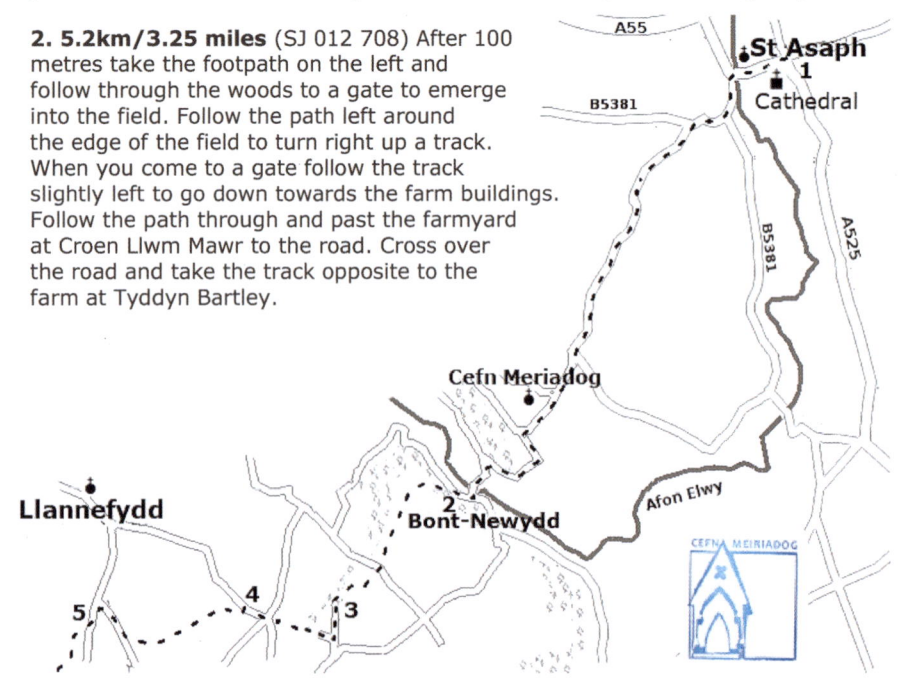

2. 5.2km/3.25 miles (SJ 012 708) After 100 metres take the footpath on the left and follow through the woods to a gate to emerge into the field. Follow the path left around the edge of the field to turn right up a track. When you come to a gate follow the track slightly left to go down towards the farm buildings. Follow the path through and past the farmyard at Croen Llwm Mawr to the road. Cross over the road and take the track opposite to the farm at Tyddyn Bartley.

The path goes between the farmhouse and the farm buildings. Go through gates and turn right after the second gate into a field. Walk along with the wood on your right to the far right-hand corner.

3. 6.9km/4.3 miles (SJ 001 699) Go over a stile into an enclosed track and turn left to go through a gate on to the lane at Ty'n y Bedw. Walk 200 metres along this lane to the first T-junction and turn right downhill towards the cottage. Passing to the left of the cottage go through this small valley over a footbridge and then up to the road. Here go right and then straight over at the crossroads.

4. 8.1km/5 miles (SH 993 698) After 150m at the footpath sign go over the stile and straight across the field to a gate. Continue through that field to the next with the hedge on your left. Go through another gate and field to a stile. You now go straight ahead across two fields then look for another stile on your right. Cross this next field diagonally to a gate, turn right and walk beside the hedge to a gate. Turn left and then immediately right onto the lane towards Llannefydd. Turn right and follow the road until you reach a fork. Take the road on the left to reach a junction.

5. 9.7km/6 miles (SH 981 699) Here you have two alternatives: to continue, turn left up the road until an area of gorse is reached on the right and take the signed footpath through it to a clearly visible stile.

Alternatively, to visit Llanefydd, turn right here and follow the road for 500m into the village. Leave the village and retrace your steps towards the footpath at the gorse.

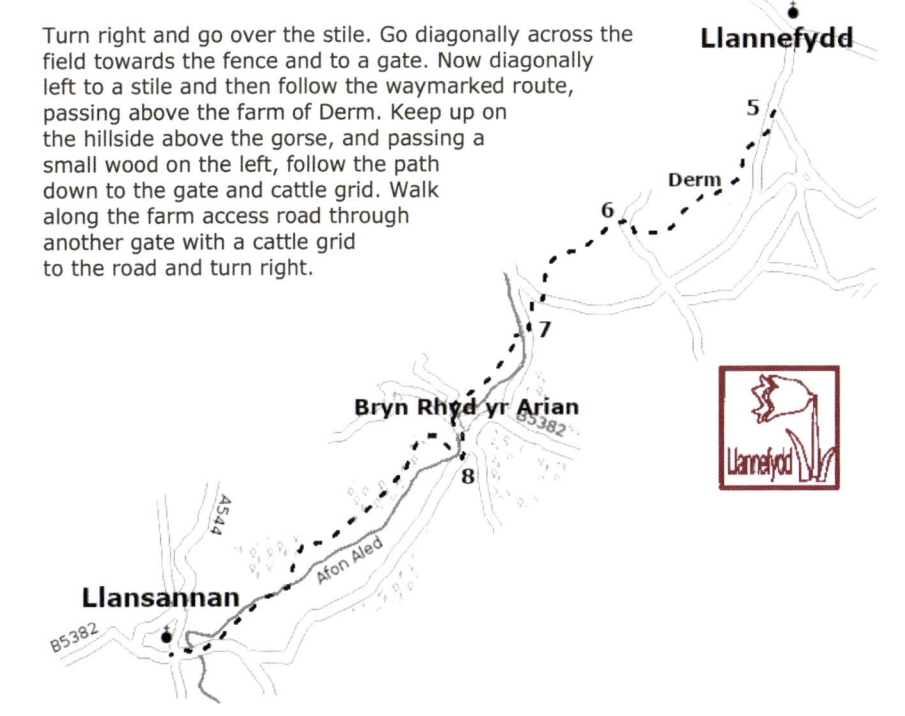

Turn right and go over the stile. Go diagonally across the field towards the fence and to a gate. Now diagonally left to a stile and then follow the waymarked route, passing above the farm of Derm. Keep up on the hillside above the gorse, and passing a small wood on the left, follow the path down to the gate and cattle grid. Walk along the farm access road through another gate with a cattle grid to the road and turn right.

23

6. 11.4km/7.1 miles (SH 969 690) At Hafodty turn left through the gate opposite. Walk down the path with the fence on your left. In the next field go diagonally left to a stile near the left-hand corner of the field. Cross over and continue with the fence on your right. Follow the waymarked route to eventually go diagonally down to a stile in the far corner of the field. Cross over to join the concrete farm track to the lane. Go over the cattle grid to turn right downhill.

7. 12.4km/7.75 miles (SH 961 683) After 50 metres take the footpath on the left down over a stile and across the stream. Pass directly in front of Cae'r Groes and, ignoring the path going off to the left, down to the lane. Go straight across to go over a stile on the right before the cottage. Go down to cross the footbridge over the river. Turn left to walk along the path with the stream on your left and the hedge on your right. Pass in front of a house to take the gate on the right on to the access track, which eventually becomes tarmac, and then to the lane. Turn left over the two bridges into the community of Bryn Rhyd yr Arian.

8. 14.0km/8.75 miles (SH 956 673) Walk past the telephone kiosk over another bridge to take the footpath immediately on your right to re-cross the river. Follow this track up through the wood. As you reach the crest the path leaves the track to go in front and past the bungalow to another track. Follow this down to cross the river once more. Immediately after crossing the river take the track right to a stile alongside a gate. Follow this track through a series of gates or over stiles to eventually reach the road. Turn right into the village of Llansannan.

Llansannan to Llangernyw

20.4km/12.75 miles
Total Ascent: 856m. **Total Descent:** 869m. Max. Elevation: 397m
Refreshments: Llansannan, Llangernyw
Toilets: Llansannan, Gwytherin, Llangernyw
Passport Stamps: Llansannan, Llangernyw churches.
OS Explorer Map 264 / OL17

Continuing along the Aled Valley – the valley of poets – and climbing to moorland before descending to Gwytherin. Up and over again to the tiny village of Pandy Tudur, then through the woods at Hafodunos (a pilgrim points the way) and into Llangernyw and a well-deserved rest and refreshment at the Stag Inn. Visit the church with its 5000 year old yew tree.

1. 0.0km/ miles (SH 934 658) From the Church, walk past the pub and the sculpture (on the right) and take the lane Ffordd Gogor on the left.

2. 0.4km/0.25 miles (SH 934 654) Just after the last house in the village and at the farmhouse of Gogor Canol take the path, left, through the farmyard. As you leave the farmyard bear right. After crossing over the bridge turn right and walk with the river also on your right over the stiles. The path enters a woodland. Follow for about 800 metres. Here the track widens slightly - look out for a path going down to the right. Take this over the footbridge. You now have a short but quite difficult and slippery climb both up and down.

(This section can be avoided by following the road and forking left after the farm - Gogor Canol - above.)

The Aled Valley is famous fo being the home of several prominent Welsh language poets: Tudur Penllyn (1420–1490), Tudur Aled (1465–1525), Sîon Tudur (1522-1602) and William Rees, commonly known in Wales by his bardic name of Gwilym Hiraethog, who was a Welsh poet and author, one of the major Welsh literary figures of the 19th century. The wooden sculpture above Cleiriach commemorates them.

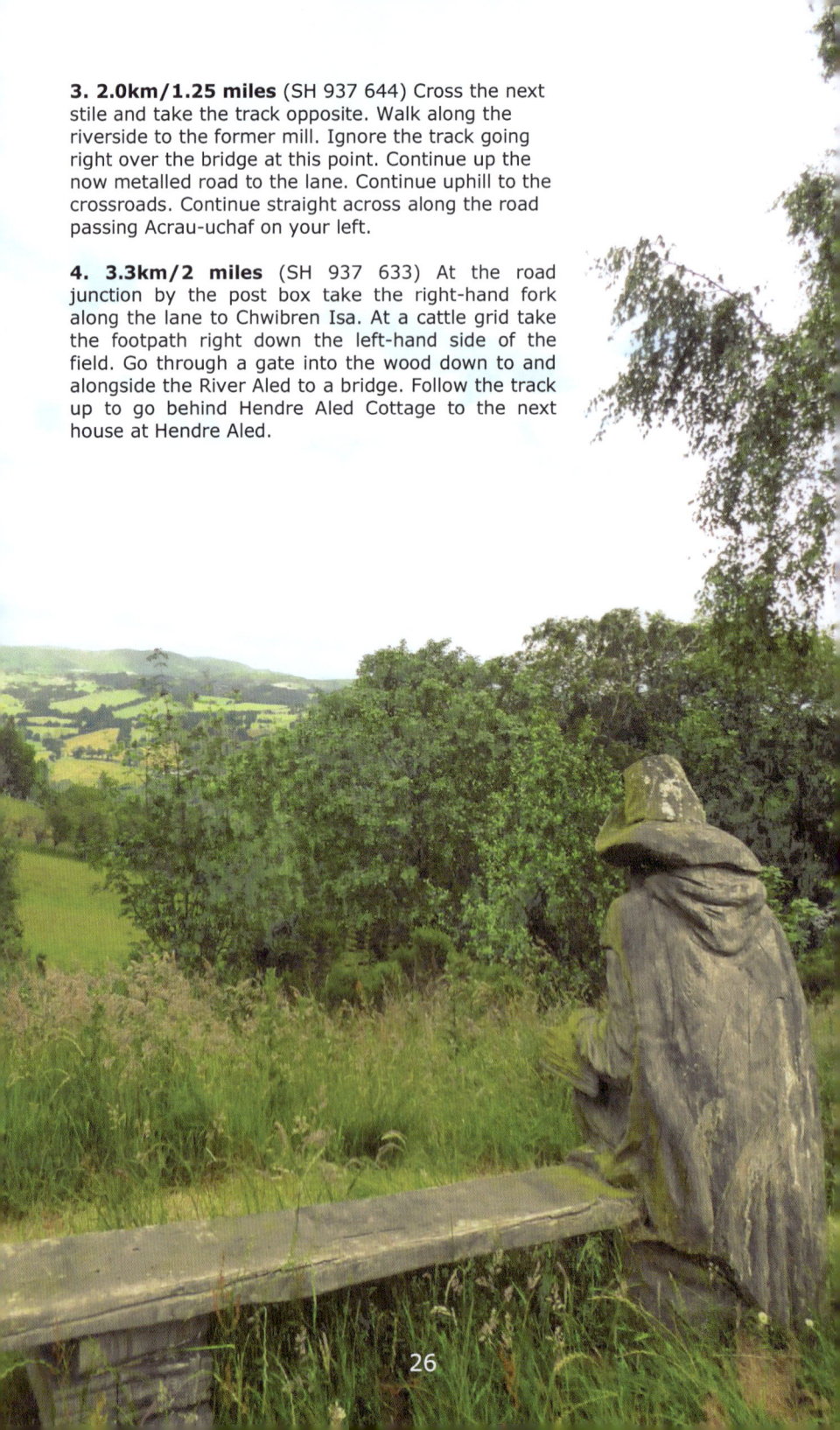

3. 2.0km/1.25 miles (SH 937 644) Cross the next stile and take the track opposite. Walk along the riverside to the former mill. Ignore the track going right over the bridge at this point. Continue up the now metalled road to the lane. Continue uphill to the crossroads. Continue straight across along the road passing Acrau-uchaf on your left.

4. 3.3km/2 miles (SH 937 633) At the road junction by the post box take the right-hand fork along the lane to Chwibren Isa. At a cattle grid take the footpath right down the left-hand side of the field. Go through a gate into the wood down to and alongside the River Aled to a bridge. Follow the track up to go behind Hendre Aled Cottage to the next house at Hendre Aled.

5. 4.7km/2.9 miles (SH 928 623) Go through and past the buildings and then take the footpath, left, through the gate with a stile alongside and into the field behind the barn. The path now goes uphill and over two stiles to the farm at Cleiriach. After the second one turn right along the farm access road which then bends to the left at the Pilgrim's Bench (a magnificent viewpoint). Follow the farm road over a cattle grid and turn right on to the Common. Turn sharp left at the T-junction and at the next T-junction turn right. Follow this lane until it bends sharply right.

6. 7.6km/4.75 miles (SH 909 618)
Go through the gate, left, and follow the track across a shallow stream and up the hill into the field. After about 70 metres, where the track goes left towards the sheep pens, leave it and go directly ahead towards a gate in the fence. Follow the path downhill with the stream alongside and to the left. Continue until you reach the derelict buildings at Hafod-gau which are in a slight dip and surrounded by trees. Go left through the gate and then another one to pass to the right of the building. Walk uphill, left, to reach a stile and cross over to the lane.

7. 8.6km/5.4 miles (SH 902 622) (Map: OS Outdoor Leisure 17) Cross over to the footpath on the other side of the lane. Walk with the fence on your left to go over two more stiles and a small footbridge. Continue directly ahead to a small ravine. Taking care, walk down to ford the stream and take the path up the other side to a stile. Continue ahead moving away from the right-hand fence to go through gap in the hedge/fence and down through two gates to the lane. Turn right along it.

8. 9.3km/5.8 miles (SH 895 622) Almost immediately turn left along the road towards the farm at Llethr. As the farm road bends to the right take the footpath, go through a kissing gate ahead, and take the stile into the field on the left. Walk with the fence on your right, keeping straight ahead when the fence bends right, down to a gate and cross a stream. With the stream on your right go slightly left uphill through a gate to walk across the field to the hedge. Continue with the hedge on your right through another field and over a stile. Go initially straight ahead but almost immediately left to go over the low hill. Bearing slightly right head for a stile and then through a gate in the fence line. Go straight across the field to a stile. Turn right to the lane.

9. 10.7km/6.7 miles (SH 883 620) Turn left down the road to the village of Gwytherin. There are two alternatives from here.

Alternative route via Pennant: The abbey where St Winefride spent her final years is reputed to be in this remote valley. Little, if anything, remains. To visit this site, take the road past the Lion Inn and up into the valley. Ignore the road going uphill and go downhill to reach another road going off to the right. This is the access road to Taipellaf. Follow this past the farm and buildings. The putative site of the abbey is marked by a large stone mound on your left. Continue up this track through gates to the lane and turn right. Take the path on the left through a gate and follow through two more gates directly ahead on to rough countryside - the path here is intermittent and indistinct. Eventually you join a fence on your left - follow this to a stile. Go over it, head for the track ahead and follow this to the road at Ty-uchaf-i'r-ffordd. Note this section is over rough country which can be extremely wet and difficult. Note too that this section is not waymarked with Pilgrim's Way markers.

The Church of St Winefride, (now privately owned) is in the centre of the village of Gwytherin opposite the Lion Inn. It was built and dedicated to her in 1869. It is believed to have been originally founded in the mid-sixth century by Prince Eleri who then established a double monastery in the valley. He was the Abbot to the monks, and his cousin's daughter, St. Winefride, eventually became the Abbess to the nuns.

10. 11.6km/7.25 miles (SH 883 620) The Main Route: Take the signposted footpath alongside the Lion Inn and beside the phone box and seat to go uphill through a wooded glade to emerge in a field. This path is indistinct and if you leave the woodland before the top walk with it (wood) to the left. Walk uphill and head for a stile to the left of Penygraig (derelict) farmhouse. Go over the stile and turn right behind the buildings to another stile onto the access track. Turn left along this to the top of the hill and where it bends right go through the gate to the track. In about 70 metres (not signed) cross over left towards the fence. Walk alongside the fence and through a kissing gate. Cross the stile in the fence to get to the road. Turn left along the lane to the junction at Ty-uchaf-i'r-ffordd. Turn right and take the lane towards the farms. After passing the entrance to Bryn Pair Uchaf follow the road until it bends to the left.

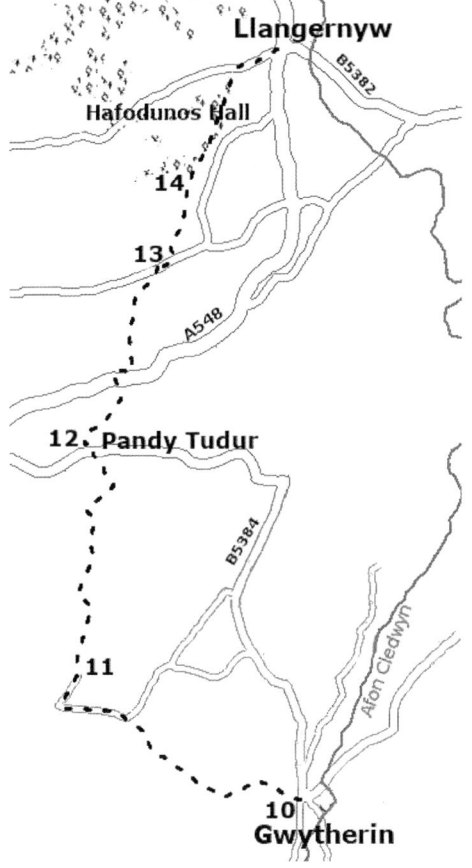

11. 14.5km/9 miles
(SH 857 624) Here go through the gate ahead. After the third gate go left alongside the hedge and through to another field to turn right. Cross the field to the far corner, go through a gate onto a track Follow this track to join the lane passing the entrance to Ty Celyn. Shortly after passing a gate on your left go over the stile, also left and follow the path through two metal kissing gates down to Pandy Tudur.

12. 16.5km/10.3 miles
(SH 858 643) Turning left, cross the bridge and then turn right up a short steep hill (marked as unsuitable for HGVs). At the top turn right along the lane towards the Old Vicarage and to the A548. Turn right and walk along this road for a short way to take the lane on the left up towards the farm at Llwyn Du Isaf. (Take care, fast traffic). At the farm go right between the farm and the farm buildings. Go through the gate into the green lane between two fields. At the top cross over a stile. Walk diagonally right across the field to a stile and then left over the next field to go through a gate to the lane.

13. 18.4km/11.5 miles
(SH 865 657) Turn right and then take the footpath in about 100 metres on the left. The path is initially a track which can be muddy. It then goes through a gate and bends right. Follow the fence for about 100 metres and at a gate (on your right) cut diagonally left and down across the field to the far corner. Here there is a ladder stile which is partially hidden by trees.

29

14. 19.1km/11.9 miles
(SH 866 663) Go over the stile and a footbridge across the stream. This path now follows the stream to the entrance to Hafodunos Hall. This section is particularly attractive and, after the second pilgrim sculpture, descends through a picturesque wooded gorge. The path, however, can be muddy, wet and slippery. At the Hafodunos Hall Lodge, turn right into the village of Llangernyw. The churchyard contains an ancient yew tree said to be between 4,000 and 5,000 years old.

Llangernyw to Rowen

18km/11 miles
Total Ascent: 640m. **Total Descent:** 736m. Max. Elevation: 303m.
Refreshments: Llangernyw, Eglwysbach, Tal-y-Cafn, Rowen
Toilets: Llangernyw, Eglwysbach, Rowen
Passport Stamps: in churches at Llangernyw, Llangelynnin, Eglwysbach, Rowen (Capel Seion)
OS Map: OL17

A steady climb out of Llangernyw and three miles of country lane before following a footpath through farmland to Eglwysbach. On tarmac again until you get to the other side of the River Conwy beyond Tal y Cafn. Crossing fields and skirting woods to eventually reach the charming village of Rowen.

1. 0.0km/ miles (SH 873 674) Retrace your steps towards Hafodunos Hall. After passing the small housing estate at Fedwen Arian on your left, take the track right past the cottage. Follow this footpath uphill, passing to the right of the derelict farmhouse of Crei. The path goes directly towards the ridge heading for the electricity pole and to a fence which you follow through gorse to a stile and then on to the hillside. Follow the path to the lane.

2. 1.7km/1 mile (SH 860 682) Turn left along this lane and follow it for 3.5km/2 miles to the junction with the B5113. Cross over to the road and follow it passing Gosen and Ty'n y Mynydd Cottage and down a steep hill.

3. 6.3km/3.9 miles (SH 820 671) After the sharp bend take the road to the right and follow this towards the Cattery at Bryn-gwian. After passing the cattery the road becomes a track which goes past a duck pond. Fork left almost immediately afterwards and then continue to go between the farmhouse and buildings at Ty Mawr. The track now turns downhill passing another house on your left. When you reach the junction of the tracks turn right uphill to Esgair Ebrill.

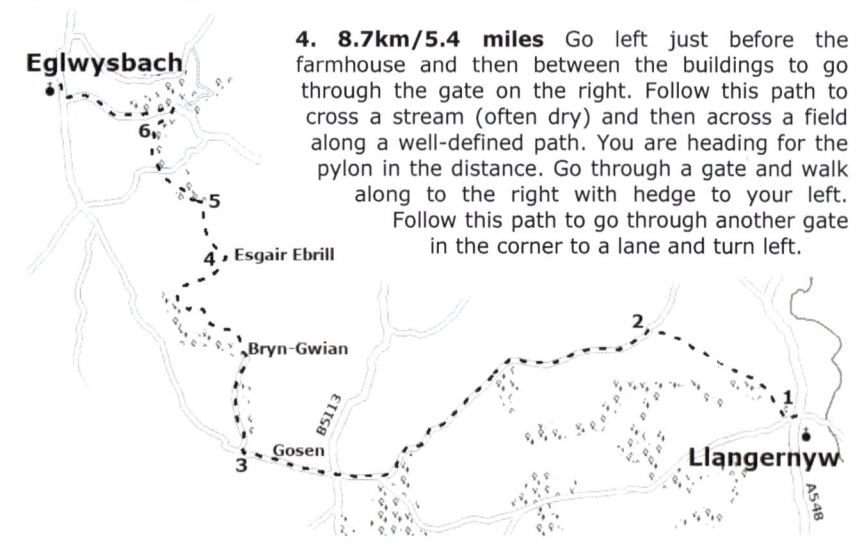

4. 8.7km/5.4 miles Go left just before the farmhouse and then between the buildings to go through the gate on the right. Follow this path to cross a stream (often dry) and then across a field along a well-defined path. You are heading for the pylon in the distance. Go through a gate and walk along to the right with hedge to your left. Follow this path to go through another gate in the corner to a lane and turn left.

5. 9.5km/5.9 miles (SH 820 671) Go downhill and through a gate to the right of the farmhouse Ty Du. Walk alongside the fence, and in about 40 metres, to go right through a walkers' gate to cross a footbridge into a wood. Follow the path through the wood and into a field. Go diagonally right uphill towards the electricity pole. Then go through a farm gate, pass the farmhouse at Llwyn Du to a lane. Cross this lane to a gated green lane. Follow this downhill until a sharp bend to the left.

6. 10.5km/6.6 miles (SH 812 701) Here, turn right up the steps and follow this narrow path up the bank through bushes into the wood. The path becomes wider and you now follow it through the wood until it eventually bends left to go down to a lane. Go left to follow this lane steeply downhill to the village of Eglwysbach.

7. 12.2km/7.6 miles (SH 802 706) After passing St Martin's Church, where the road bends slightly to the right take the narrow lane to the left to go over the stream. Turn right at the junction and continue to the road. Turn left and go left again when the road forks. This road leads to the crossroads at Tal-y-cafn.

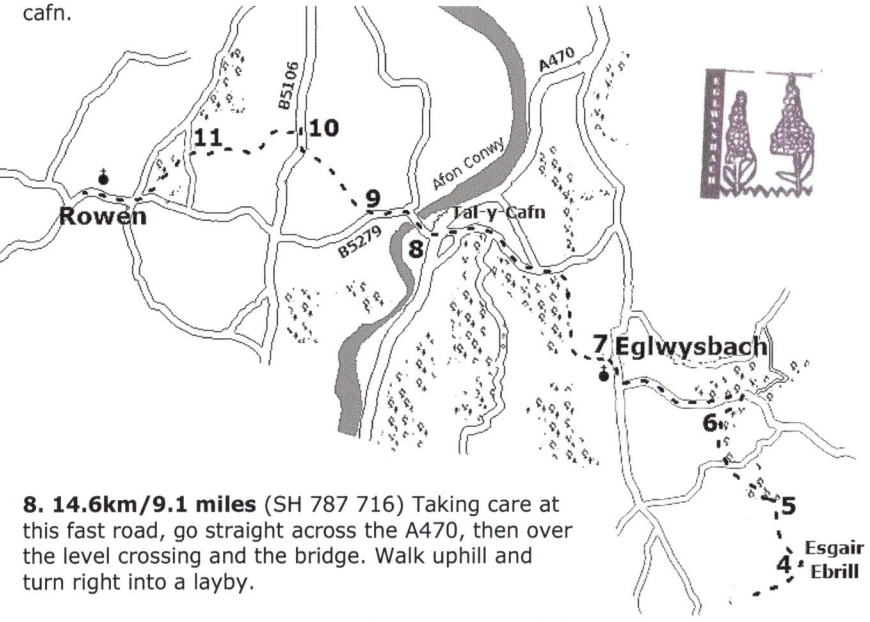

8. 14.6km/9.1 miles (SH 787 716) Taking care at this fast road, go straight across the A470, then over the level crossing and the bridge. Walk uphill and turn right into a layby.

(To go to the Conwy Valley Barn bunkhouse turn left at the small housing estate and follow the path alongside the river.)

9. 15.3km/9.6 miles (SH 782 718) Take the footpath that goes left and follow it through several fields and ladder stiles to the main road. Turn right and, taking care, walk alongside the B5106. In 160m take the next footpath on the left, down through a metal ladder stile.

10. 16.2km/10.1 miles (SH 776 725) Take this path, which can be quite wet and muddy, towards the farm. Walk through the two gates to the farm. Pass to the right of the farmhouse and then right through another gate. Go ahead and through to the next field. Turn left and walk with the hedge on your left to go over a stile into another field. Walk slightly downhill and head for the gate on your right. Go through this and directly across to go through another gate. Continue directly ahead and uphill to go through a gate to the left of a small copse and pick up a track. Follow this track to the farm buildings at Glyn Uchaf. Turn left to go through this farmyard between the house and the farm buildings. Follow the farm drive to the lane.

11. 17.5km/10.9 miles (SH 765 722) Cross over the lane and go through the kissing gate. The path goes directly ahead passing to the left of the trees in the distance. Continue now with the hedge on your right to go over two ladder stiles to the lane. Turn right to walk into Rowen.

Rowen to Abergwyngregyn

16.8km / 10.5 miles
Total Ascent: 946m. **Total Descent:** 922m. Max Elevation: 402m.
Refreshments: Rowen Pub, Llanfairfechan, Abergwyngregyn.
Toilets: Rowen, Llanfairfechan, Abergwyngregyn (top car park)
Passport Stamps: Rowen (Capel Seion), Abergwyngreygn (Caffi Hen Felin)
OS Map: OL17

A steep climb through the woods on the Coffin Path to the ancient little church at Llangelynnin with its walled baptismal well in the corner of the churchyard. Continuing up into the foothills of the Carneddau, passing ancient stone circles before dropping down to Llanfairfechan. Up again to meet the Roman road that descends to Abergwyngregyn.

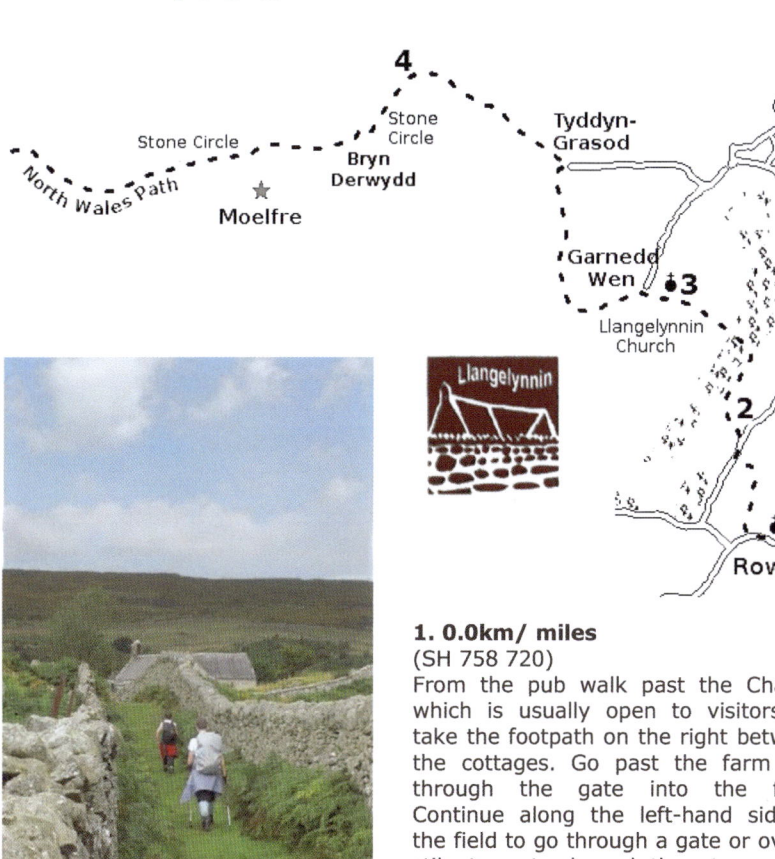

1. 0.0km/ miles
(SH 758 720)
From the pub walk past the Chapel, which is usually open to visitors, to take the footpath on the right between the cottages. Go past the farm and through the gate into the field. Continue along the left-hand side of the field to go through a gate or over a stile to a track and then turn right. When this track bends to the right cross over a stile ahead and walk again along the left-hand side of the field. Cross over a stile and walk up the well-defined path directly up to a gate on to the lane. Turn right along the lane.

2. 0.9km/0.6 miles (SH 757 727) At Llwyn On, leave the lane and take the farm drive on your left. This leads to a large and steep ladder stile on the right. Go into the field and diagonally across it to a gate. Go through the gate and, with the wall on your right, head towards the cottage. Cross over the stone footbridge to the lane. Enter the wood and walk directly ahead. When you reach the track coming from the road turn left uphill. You are now on an ancient "Coffin Path" which leads eventually to the little church at Llangelynnin.

3. 2.4km/1.5 miles (SH 751 736) From this little church continue around the outside wall to take the track going left uphill on to the open countryside. Take the right-hand path, aim for the end of the wall in the distance and after crossing the stream at the fords, take the path that keeps close to the wall on your right. At this point you have broad views over the Conwy Valley, Conwy Town and Castle. When you reach the sheep pens at Tyddyn-grasod, turn left along the path to go over the open land (aim slightly to the right of the flat-topped hill in the distance). Continue straight on, ignoring paths on left and right, and when you come to the brow walk ahead towards a clump of trees within a wall and pass these to the right. The path now joins the North Wales Path at a waymarker post. Go straight ahead and down to the stream. Cross over the footbridge and follow the path up to a waymarker post and then go left.

(For Penmaenmawr go to the wall, climb the ladder stile and follow the tracks and waymarked route down to the town).

4. 5.7km/3.6 miles (SH 733 753) Follow the path to a gate in a wall and turn left to join the Wales Coast Path. The North Wales Path and Wales Coast Path now follow the same route. Continue to follow the waymarked path for 1.2km/0.75 miles past Bryn Derwedd on your right to the complex of stone circles on your left high above the town of Penmaenmawr.

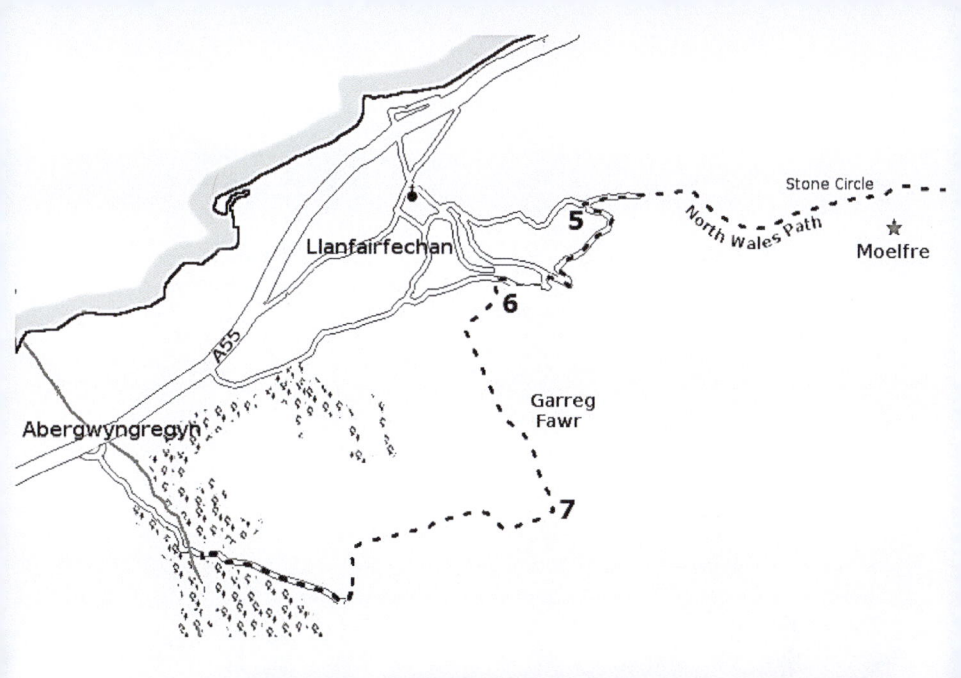

To join from Penmaenmawr, start from the car park behind the Library off Bangor Road. Go up the steps to the left of the flats and at the top of the steps turn right then veer left (ignore the first stone track on your left). Now follow the lane with houses on your right along the edge of the playing field and on to the road. Turn left and then right at the first footpath past the cottages (conversion of the old Craiglwyd Farm) to rejoin the North Wales Path and the Wales Coast Path at the distinctive slate marker post.

After visiting the Stone Circles return to the main path and follow it westwards to a marker post where the Wales Coast Path leaves right to go down to Llanfairfechan. Now continue ahead on the waymarked North Wales Path which eventually goes past a farm and follows the farm track to a tarmac lane. Continue ahead down the lane to a T-junction.

5. 9.9km/6.2 miles (SH 695 746) Turn left and follow the road down to the entrance to Nant y Coed Nature Reserve. *(To go to Llanfairfechan, turn right and follow the road to the centre of this small former market town.)* Staying on the North Wales Path, cross the stream and bear right following the road (Valley Road) to join Terrace Walk. Ignore the first footpath on the left and continue to reach a metal kissing gate on your left.

6. 11.7km/7.3 miles (SH 688 740) Turn left and follow the path which now climbs steadily uphill to reach a metal kissing gate in a wall. The path continues uphill for another 0.5km/0.3 mile crossing open land to eventually reach a large stone at the Roman Road.

7. 13.8km/8.6 miles (SH 693 722) Turn right to follow this ancient route down to a small car park. Follow the road down to the bridge in the forest at Abergwyngregyn. The village is about a kilometre down the road.

Abergwyngregyn to Bangor Cathedral

19.6km / 12.25 miles
Total Ascent: 533m. **Total Descent:** 596m. Max. Elevation: 287m.
Refreshments: Abergwyngregyn, Bangor
Toilets: Abergwygregyn (top car park), Bangor
Passport Stamps: Abergwyngregyn (Caffi Hen Felin), Bangor Cathedral, Trespass Outdoor shop (Bangor).
OS Map: OL17

After visiting the magnificent waterfall, the path winds around the edge of the hills overlooking the coast, with views across to Bangor and Penrhyn Castle towards Anglesey. Then on through country lanes and farmland, passing the medieval hall house Cochwillan, dropping down to cross the River Ogwen, passing under the A55, leading to an old rail track through woodland and into Bangor.

Having descended to the bridge (Bont Newydd on the map) and if you do not wish to visit the village of Abergwyngregyn, turn left before the bridge to follow the North Wales Path (NWP) and walk up the road to the car park.

1. 0.0km/ miles (SH 662 720) Just before the car park take the path on the right signed "Waterfalls" and go over the bridge. Follow this path for 2.1km/ 1.25 miles to the waterfalls. The NWP goes past another waterfall and then climbs slowly around the side of the hill. After passing under the powerlines you will shortly arrive at a seat with wide views over Ynys Mon, the Great Orme and beyond to North West England. Continue to follow the NWP to go under the powerlines again – and then for a third time. The path now crosses several streams and you eventually reach a gate at a fence and wall. Continue along the main path which winds along until you pass a wooded area on your right (Nant Heilyn). Continue along the well-marked path through a gate by another wooded area (Coed Bronydd Isaf) and after another 300m, the track will lead you out onto a lane.

2. 9.2km/5.75 miles (SH 626 704) Turn left and walk along the lane. Ignore the road going downhill right. When you arrive at the powerline take the footpath right towards Plas Uchaf. Go through the kissing gate and past the farm. Cross the next field along a green track towards the woods. At the pylon and gorse bushes turn left along a footpath, with the wall on your right, heading towards another pylon. Cross the stream to go around the bank to the track. Turn right and walk to the next gate at a track. Cross over to the remains of a stone stile and walk with the wall on your right. Just before the next house go left over a stile. Take the next stile on your right on to the access road, turn left along it to the lane.

3. 11.1km/6.9 miles (SH 616 695) Go left up the lane for 40m until you reach a stile in the wall on your right. You are still following the North Wales Path and you should still be looking for those markers as well as any Pilgrims Way markers. Continue across the field with the wall on your right. When you reach a gate in the wall beside some old buildings, bear left following the track up into a field surrounded by gorse. Turn right and keeping the gorse on your right, find a path through the gorse which will lead to a stile by a small stream. Cross the metal stile, then cross a wall. Continue (keeping the wall to your right) going through two kissing gates to reach a lane.

4. 11.8km/7.4 miles (SH 613 689) Here turn right along it for about 1km/0.6 mile until you see a left turn to the medieval hall house, Plas Cochwillan. Bearing right alongside this wonderful medieval hall house, go along the track towards the woods.

Cochwillan was built around 1465 by William ap Gruffudd who, for supporting Henry Tudor at the Battle of Bosworth, was rewarded by being named Sheriff of Caernarvonshire. In the 17th century John Williams, Archbishop of York combined the hall with the Penrhyn estate. By 1969 it was in use as a barn when it was restored by Cadw and the Penrhyn estate.

40

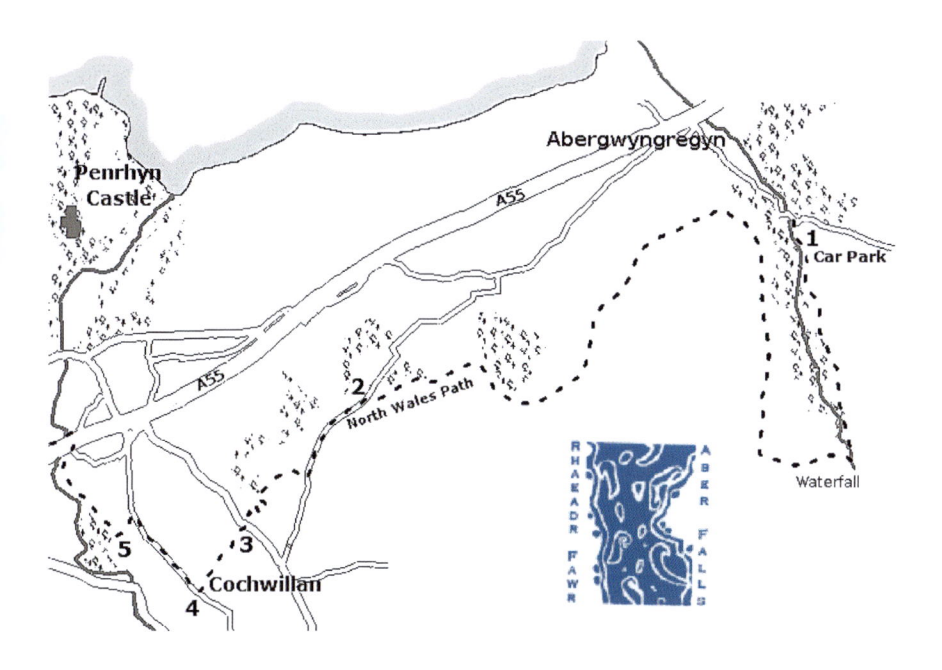

5. 12.9km/8 miles (SH 606 693) Turn right through the kissing gate and walk along the edge of the woods. Follow the path down until eventually you will see the river on your left, before arriving at the watermill. Turn left at the mill and follow the path across the river coming out onto a track/lane. Go right here to go under the A55. The access road bends left then right to become metalled. Follow this, passing the rugby club ground on your left, and continue straight down the lane.

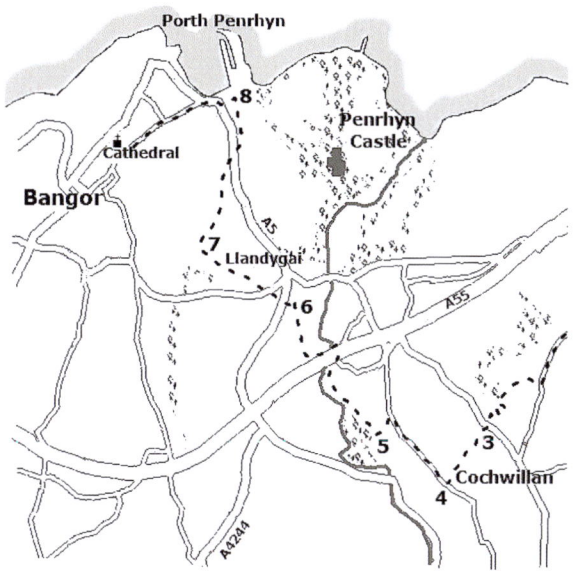

6. 14.7km/9.2 miles (SH 597 706) Turn left at the first turning. Here you join the Wales Coast Path. Go to the right through the bushes to follow the path to a bus-stop on a major road. Cross the road to a footpath which runs by the railway air shaft that looks like a small castle turret. This path goes to another lane which you cross to another path which takes you down by the side of an industrial park. When you get to a roadway, turn left and go down to the end of the road and then through some barriers.

41

7. 15.9km/9.9 miles (SH 588 711) Turn right to join the old railway track into Porth Penrhyn.

8. 17.5km/10.9 miles
(SH 592 725) Arriving at the Port, turn left and follow the Wales Coast Path over the bridge and up the hill to the A5 road. Cross this with care and go through the bollards into Penybryn Road. Follow the road underneath a stone bridge and at the end turn left into the High Street. Walk down the street all the way to Bangor City Centre and the Cathedral.

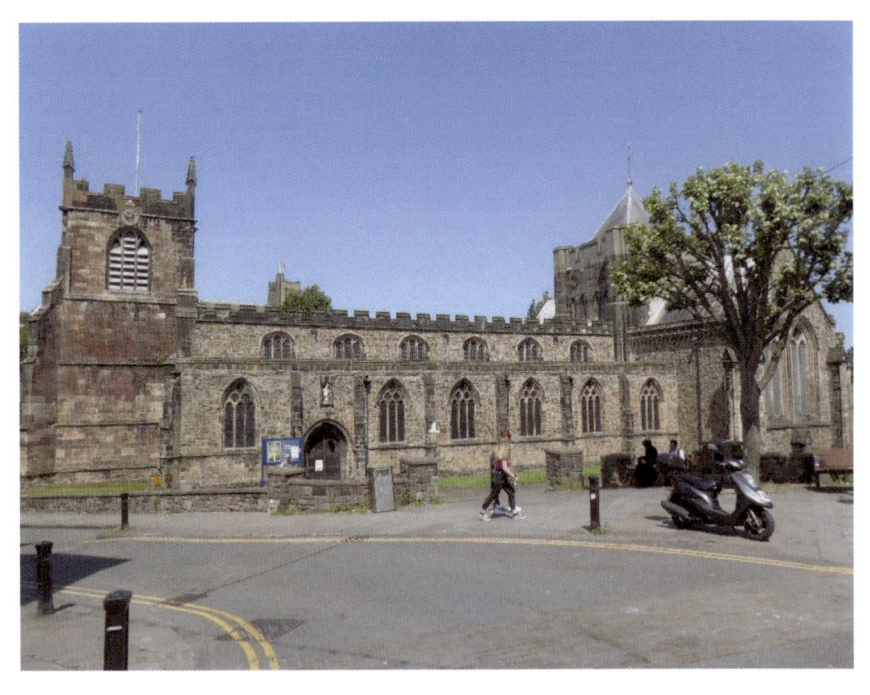

Bangor Cathedral, dedicated to St Deiniol, stands on land given to the saint by the king of Gwynedd in the middle of the 6th century. Deiniol is said to have been consecrated Bishop of Bangor by St David. Like St Asaph Cathedral the current building suffered at the hands of both Edward I and Owain Glyndwr and like St David's Cathedral, it was built in a low-lying area in an attempt to escape the attention of Viking raiders. The building was much restored in the 1860's.

Bangor Cathedral to Llanberis

17.6km / 11 miles
Total Ascent: 1003m. Total Descent: 923m. Max. Elevation: 360m.
Refreshments: Bangor, Tregarth, Llanberis
Toilets: Bangor, Llanberis
Passport Stamps: Bangor Cathedral, Trespass Outdoor shop (Bangor), Pant Gwyn cottage, Llanberis (Joe Brown's)
OS Map: OL17

Over Bangor Mountain (a hill really) to follow another old rail track to former slate quarrying villages, over moorland and down through the oak wooded Padarn Country Park to Llanberis.

As an alternative, to avoid the mountain route, you can follow the Wales Coast Path through Y Felinheli and Caernarfon all the way to Clynnog Fawr.

1. 0.0km/ miles (SH 580 720) Leaving the Cathedral, continue along the High Street until you find a path that goes off to the left just past a chapel and before you reach the Lidl store.

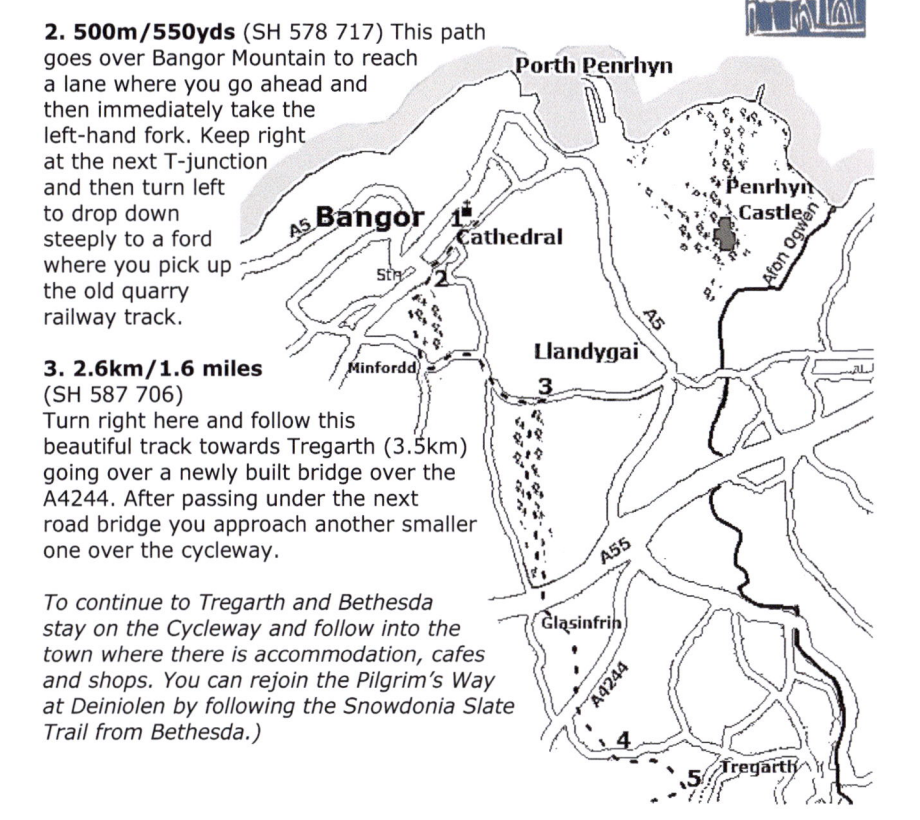

2. 500m/550yds (SH 578 717) This path goes over Bangor Mountain to reach a lane where you go ahead and then immediately take the left-hand fork. Keep right at the next T-junction and then turn left to drop down steeply to a ford where you pick up the old quarry railway track.

3. 2.6km/1.6 miles (SH 587 706) Turn right here and follow this beautiful track towards Tregarth (3.5km) going over a newly built bridge over the A4244. After passing under the next road bridge you approach another smaller one over the cycleway.

To continue to Tregarth and Bethesda stay on the Cycleway and follow into the town where there is accommodation, cafes and shops. You can rejoin the Pilgrim's Way at Deiniolen by following the Snowdonia Slate Trail from Bethesda.)

4. 5.9km/3.7 miles (SH 596 679) Walk up the path to the left of this bridge and turn right to go over it. Follow this path to a group of buildings (old hamlet of Pandy).

5. 6.3km/3.9 miles (SH 599 676) At the buildings turn right along a track which quickly becomes a footpath alongside a low ridge. When you come to another track cross over it to go through a walkers' gate. When you arrive at the Woodland Trust go left through the gate. Follow this footpath, bearing right uphill, to the lane.

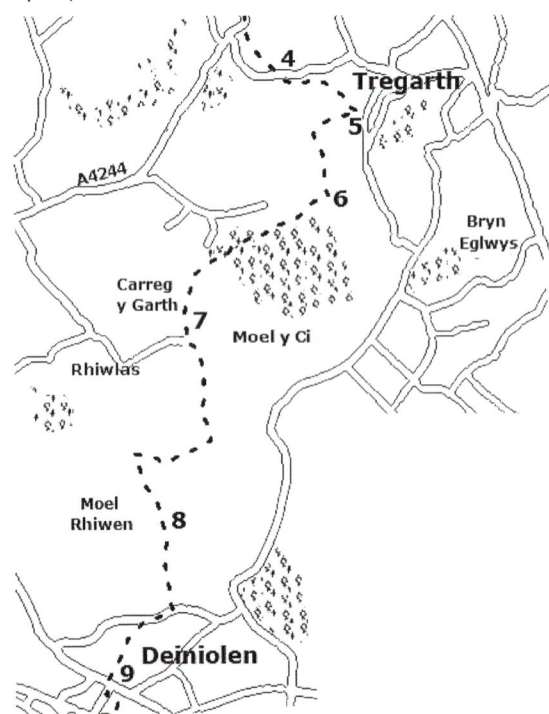

6. 7.2km/4.5 miles (SH 596 669) Turn right along the lane. At the staggered junction, bear left to follow the metalled lane and just before you reach a gated driveway, turn left into the woods. Follow this path up through the woods to a wall where you turn right to follow with the wall on your left. At the kissing gate turn left through the gap in the wall and continue through the woods until you come to a kissing gate in a wall. Go through it and with the wall on your right follow the path round the side of Moel-y-Ci to another gate which leads out onto a track. Turn left along it to reach the top of the hill at Tynllidiart.

7. 9.0km/5.6 miles (SH 585 658) Here the metalled lane drops to the right. Then take the second path on the left through a gate. This path/lane passes through two farms at Cae'r Gof. Go ahead through three walls. After the last one, go left uphill to go through the wall on to the Common. Walk with wall on your right to a gate to leave the Common. Go directly across the field and down and across the stream. Continue uphill until the footpath bends sharply left. This leads to a derelict farmhouse, Maes Meddygon.

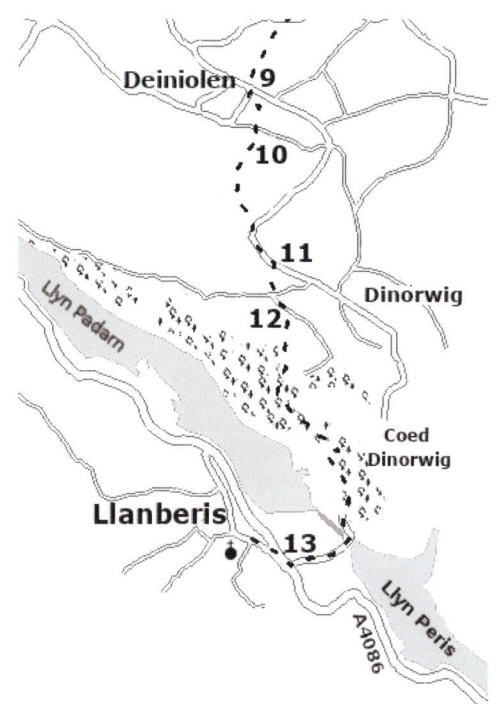

8. 10.8km/6.75 miles
(SH 581 647) Pass to the right of and behind the ruins to reach open land again. Continue over the hillside and down to the road at Ffridd Uchaf. Turn right and take the second footpath on the left and follow this path down to the main road and turn left into the High Street.

9. 12.8km/8 miles
(SH 579 632) At the road junction turn right down New Street. Go past the shop to the next road junction. Here turn left into Tai Caradog with a stone wall separating the road from the sheltered housing on your right. Walk along to the end and where the road bends to the left, take the footpath through the kissing gate on your right. Go through this and continue past the houses to cross a stream with its two footbridges to a lane.

45

10. 13.2km/8.25 miles (SH 579 629) Turn left and after a few metres take the next footpath on your right. Go right where the path forks and follow to the top of the hill and turn left along the access road to another road and turn right.

11. 14.3km/8.9 miles (SH 581 619) Follow this road to the houses at Maes Eilian and before the bus shelter take the footpath right. When you reach the next lane cross it to another lane.

12. 14.8km/9.25 miles (SH 582 616) Take the footpath immediately after the cottage Pant Gwyn (stamp here and possibly a cup of tea if you knock) down an access road on your right. This enters the wood of Padarn Country Park and the path is easy to follow down through the wood. On leaving the wood turn left along the road to meet the road from the Quarry Hospital Museum. Cross over this road to go over a footbridge and follow this path with the railway on your left to the main road.

13. 17.3km/10.8 miles (SH 581 599) Turn right, then cross over the road and turn right into the High Street of Llanberis.

The Quarry Hospital Museum - The pioneering Dinorwig Quarry Hospital is now a museum housing some of the original equipment from the 1800's: Restored Ward and Operating Theatre, original X-Ray Machine, other bits of gruesome medical equipment and a Mortuary! This old hospital in Llanberis was for the men who worked at the Dinorwig Quarry in the 19th and 20th centuries. The idea was to have a hospital close to their place of work so they could get back to work as soon as possible after they received treatment.

Llanberis to Penygroes

18.6km / 11.6 miles
Total Ascent: 684m. **Total Descent:** 698m. Max. Elevation: 378m.
Refreshments: Llanberis, Waenfawr, Penygroes
Toilets: Llanberis, Waenfawr, Penygroes
Passport Stamps: Llanberis (Joe Brown's), Penygroes (Llun Mewn Ffram – Gallery and framing shop on Snowdon St.)
OS Map: OL17

Some good hill walking today, with a chance to pause at the community pub by the station in Waenfawr, before climbing again in the foothills of Snowdonia, passing old slate quarry workings, deep, water filled pits and a stroll alongside a stream into Penygroes.

1. 0.0km/ miles (SH 578 600) From the Parish Church at Llanberis walk towards the centre of the village. Within 100m turn left into Capel Coch Road signposted to the Youth Hostel. After passing the Chapel on your left turn right and then left uphill. Follow this road out into the open country.

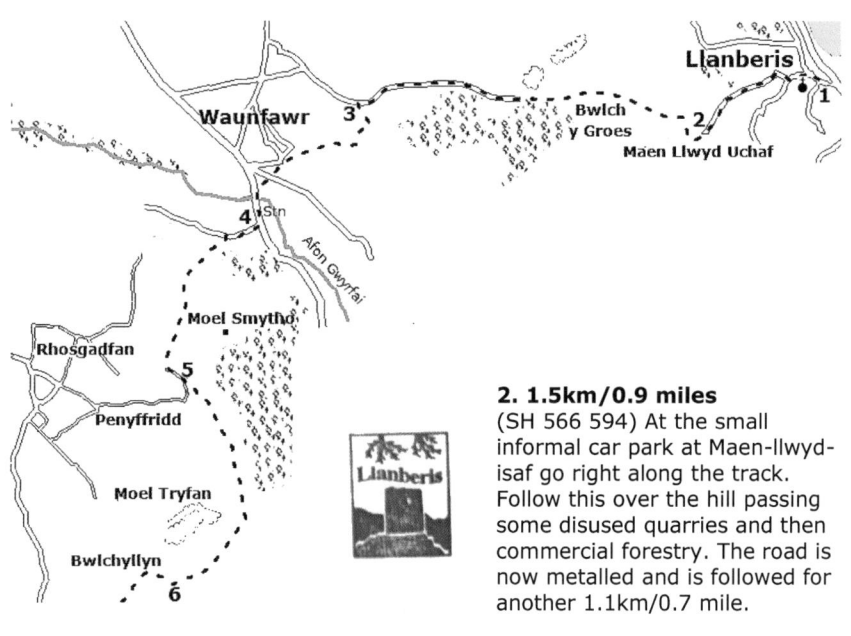

2. 1.5km/0.9 miles
(SH 566 594) At the small informal car park at Maen-llwyd-isaf go right along the track. Follow this over the hill passing some disused quarries and then commercial forestry. The road is now metalled and is followed for another 1.1km/0.7 mile.

3. 5.0km/3.1 miles (SH 535 598) Just after it bends to the right take the footpath (access road) on the left at Hafod Oleu to follow the dragonfly waymarkers. Pass two cottages on the left and just after the ford take the path to the right downhill with a stream on the right. In the larger field turn right along the footpath which now makes its way through many small fields following the Hafod Oleu (dragonfly) waymarks to Bryn y Pystill at Waunfawr. Follow the lane to a minor road and housing estate, turn right and then in 90m/100yds turn left through a kissing gate down a hedged path to the main road and turn left.

4. 7.0km/4.4 miles (SH 526 587) Follow the main road over the river and past the community run Snowdonia Inn. Take the lane on the right signposted Rhosgadfan. Follow this to pick up a path going left (signposted Y Fron) to cross a stream. It then climbs up over two ladder stiles on to the Common. (The ruins of an old farming community are a great place to stop and enjoy the view.) Go straight ahead towards the left-hand corner of the sheepfolds. The path goes alongside this wall and passes two dwellings on your right to join the track towards Hafod Rhuffydd Farm where a metalled road is now joined. Follow this until it bends to the right.

5. 9.2km/5.75 miles (SH 519 571)
Here take the footpath going left - there is a waymarker post a little way along this path. The path is now waymarked across the moorland. You come to a junction of paths, marked by an extremely large stone to the right. Turn right towards it and follow the path to the left of it past the waste tips for the disused Moel Tryfan Slate Quarry. There are good views of the Nantlle ridge and the lake below.

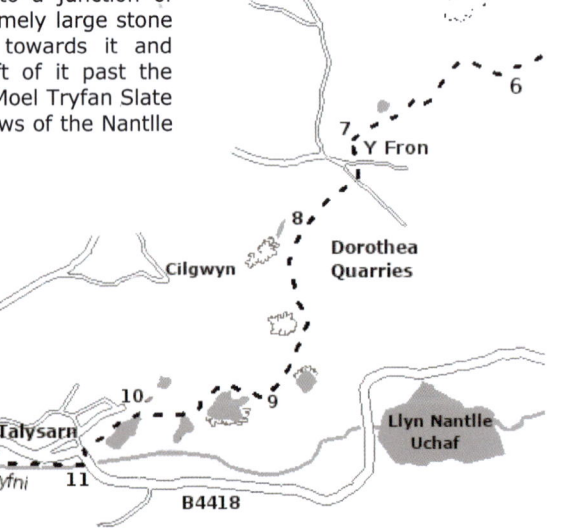

6. 11.4km/7.1 miles (SH 518 554) The path now goes right into the quarry and joins the access road which is followed around to a cattle grid. Go over and take the right fork. Follow the path past another disused and flooded quarry.

7. 12.6km/7.9 miles (SH508 550) After leaving the edge of the quarry go through a kissing gate and follow the track downhill with a recently rebuilt stone wall on your right. At a farm gate signed Bethel on your right, take the footpath opposite through a kissing gate with Slate Trail marker. Follow the path down between two fields, through another kissing gate to a lane. Turn right at the footpath sign on to Cae Fron and then left at the bus shelter following the footpath signed Slate Trail. The community centre and bunkhouse are on your right. Follow the footpath around to a lane and turn right and then immediately left into the field through a kissing gate. Go straight across to another kissing gate following the path over the open ground and up some steps onto a track, turning left.

8. 13.6km/8.5 miles (SH503 542) On coming to a gate keep left, walking around the perimeter with the fence on your right. Follow the footpath when it veers away to the left, through a kissing gate and onto the path below the piles of slate waste, and in 20m go through the kissing gate on your left and cross the field to the bottom right-hand corner and another kissing gate. There are extensive slate workings all around ahead of you as you descend into the valley, together with glimpses of Snowdon and Llyn Nantlle Uchaf. Turn left through the gate at a sign showing the footpaths in Dorothea Quarry and continue downhill towards, and then through, another kissing gate leading onto a narrow path around the edge of a slate tip. The path is quite narrow as it goes around the edge of one of the tips with quite a steep, though short, drop to your left. Follow the Slate Trail signs as the path zigzags through the quarry workings on a well-defined track.

9. 14.9km/9.3 miles (SH 502 533) On reaching a T junction with another track turn right, ignoring the Slate Trail marker pointing left. At a fork keep to the right on the main track skirting the north side of the large Dorothea Quarry lake, passing the overgrown ruins of Talysarn Hall to your right. Stay on this track until you reach a small roundabout with trees in the middle. Take the left fork and continue down the lane to a kissing gate on your left.

10. 15.8km/9.9 miles (SH 491 531) Go through the kissing gate and turn right to follow the path onto a track that soon goes past the football ground on your left. Follow the path to a kissing gate onto the road where you turn left. Cross the road onto the opposite footpath and follow the road until you see a footpath sign on your right.

11. 16.6km/10.4 miles (SH 489 528) Walk down this pleasant footpath through the trees with a stream on your left. When you reach a footbridge do not cross it but turn right onto the riverside path with the Afon Llyfni on your left. Follow this path carefully through two kissing gates. After the second gate the path turns gradually to the right across a raised slate causeway that eventually rises up to a kissing gate onto the main road (B4418). Turn left and cross over the road with care and take the wide footpath opposite and follow it all the way into Penygroes.

Penygroes to Trefor

16.7km / 10.4 miles
Total Ascent:442m. **Total Descent:**522m. Max. Elevation: 142m.
Refreshments: Penygroes, Clynnog Fawr, Trefor
Toilets: Penygroes, Clynnog Fawr, Trefor (Y Tŵr)
Passport Stamps: Penygroes (Llun Mewn Ffram – Gallery and framing shop on Snowdon St.), Clynnog Fawr (church), Trefor (Village Shop)
OS Map: OL17

A gentle day through farmland with views of the three peaks of Yr Eifl and the sea. Some road walking and a stop at the pilgrims' church of St Beuno at Clynnog Fawr. There is a choice to walk along the beach to Trefor if the tide is out.

1. 0.0km/ miles (SH 470 530) From the centre of Penygroes turn into Snowdon Street and follow it into Market Place and left into Station Road then right into Clynnog Road. Cross the footbridge over the A487 and straight over the cycleway to follow the road, Ffordd Clynnog, round to the right past the houses. At the T-junction turn right on to a road.

2. 830m/0.5 miles (SH 462 528) Opposite the metal fence of the Penygroes Quarry take the kissing gate into the field. Walk across the field with the gorse hedge on your right. At the end of the field turn right to a gate following the track through the derelict farm buildings and down to the lane.

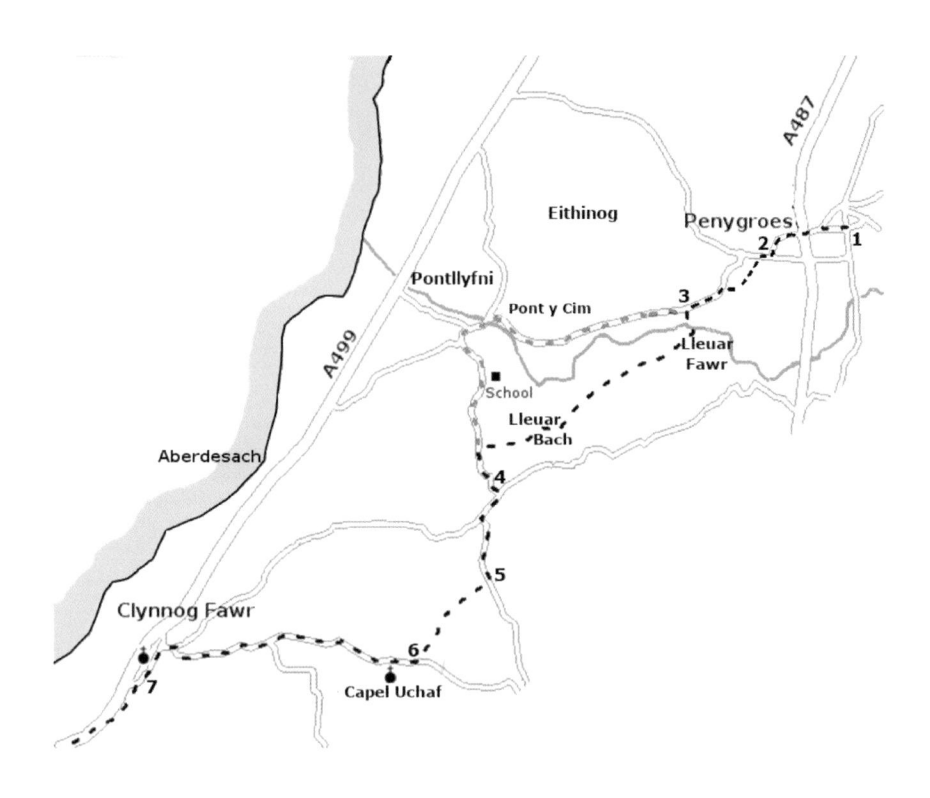

3. 1.55km/1 mile. (SH 457 524) Take the next farm track on the left on to a bridleway, but signposted as a footpath, passing The Woollen Mill self-catering cottages to your right. Cross over the footbridge and follow the path to the right to join the access road to Lleuar Fawr. Go between the farmhouse and the farmyard to go towards the gates ahead and go through on the righthand side. Continue along the footpath to Lleuar Bach. Turn right towards the farm and almost immediately go left through a small gate before the wall. Walk alongside the large barn to a gate into a large field. Cross this field to go through a gate and turn right. Follow the fence to the hedge and turn left walking with the hedge and then the fence on the right. Go through the gate which is a little way to the left of the fence and then continue to walk with the fence on your right past Ty'n y Rhôs. By now the fence is a new hedge. Continue with this still on your right to go through gate on to a green track. Go through another gate and turn left along the lane.

4. 4.45km/2.8 miles (SH 442 510) Turn right at the first T-junction and left (uphill) along another lane.

5. 5.24km/3.3 miles (SH 441 503) The lane soon goes downhill and at the bottom take the footpath on your right over a footbridge alongside a ford. Walk along the lane to go through wooden gate to the left of the house. Walk straight uphill with the hedge to your left. Continue through another two gates to enter the farmyard at Bryn Hafod. Go between the buildings and down the farm drive to the road.

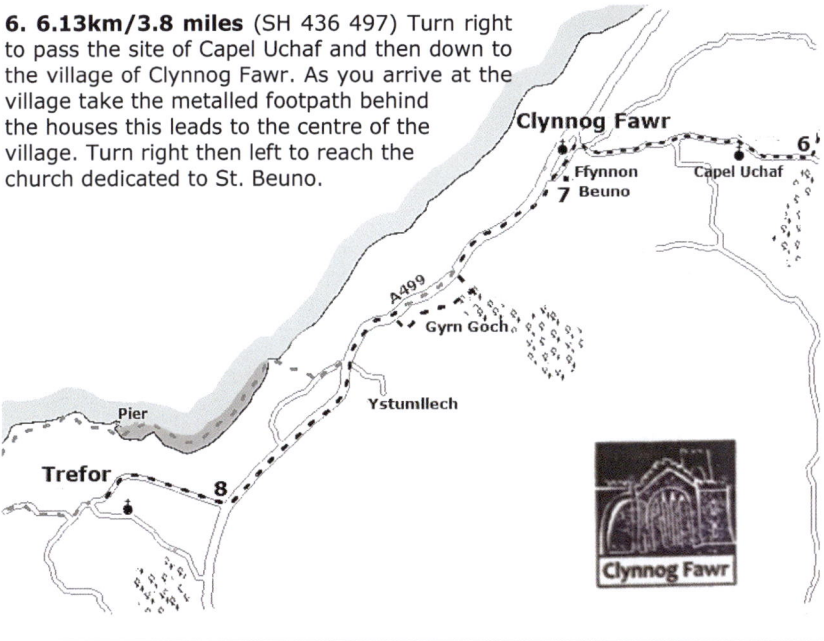

6. 6.13km/3.8 miles (SH 436 497) Turn right to pass the site of Capel Uchaf and then down to the village of Clynnog Fawr. As you arrive at the village take the metalled footpath behind the houses this leads to the centre of the village. Turn right then left to reach the church dedicated to St. Beuno.

7. 8.7km/5.4 miles (SH 413 495) Leave the village by following the old road (now a cycleway) past Ffynnon Beuno (St. Beuno's Well). The cycleway goes alongside the A499 and is also waymarked as the Wales Coast Path. Continue along it (just over ½ mile) to Pont y Felin and turn left up a footpath into the wood at Gyrn Goch. Cross over a footbridge and continue right uphill. At a fork in the path turn right (slightly downhill) to go over a stile in a stone wall. Follow the path through bracken with the wall on your right before bending left uphill to a gate in a wall. Follow the path downhill to a track leading to a lane. Follow this to the A499. Turn left along the cycle track until you see the white gate for Rock Cottage on your left.

8. 13.3km/8.3 miles (SH 384 466) Continue a short way until at a waymarker post, the path goes right to cross the A499 and then go down the road signed directly into the village of Trefor.

Alternatively, and only at low tide, leave the Coast Path at the entrance of Ystumllech and take the lane on the opposite side of the road. In about 300 metres take the footpath right. At the house Tal Eryr take the path left behind it which leads down to the beach. You can now walk along the beach into the village of Trefor.

Check the tide tables and ensure you have enough time.

Trefor to Nefyn

10.4km / 6.5 miles *(15.5km / 9.7 miles by alternative coastal route)*
Total Ascent: 620m. Total Descent: 583m. Max.
Elevation: 349m.
Refreshments: Trefor, Nefyn
Toilets: Trefor (Y Tŵr), Nefyn
Passport Stamps: Trefor (shop), Pistyll church, Nefyn (Maritime Museum).
OS Explorer Map 254/253

A start to test your energy levels with a steep climb up to the Bwlch yr Eifl with spectacular views up and down the coast before descending over farmland to the pretty church at Pistyll, a good place for a picnic. Continue on pleasant footpaths to Nefyn.

There are two possible routes here:

Inland Route via Trefor:

1. 0.0km/ miles (SH 339 436) At the village centre, with the shop on your left, the through road bears left - ignore this and go straight across and ahead along an unnamed street. Pass over a bridge with Capel Bethania on the right and car park on the left. At the end of the houses turn left, up a lane, climbing steadily.

2. 0.73km/0.5 miles (SH 368 462) When the lane turns sharp left continue ahead up a track (which becomes a path) to Bwlch yr Eifl. On reaching a gravel vehicle track descending from the quarry workings seen to your right, bear left to follow this track down to the car park for Nant Gwrtheyrn.

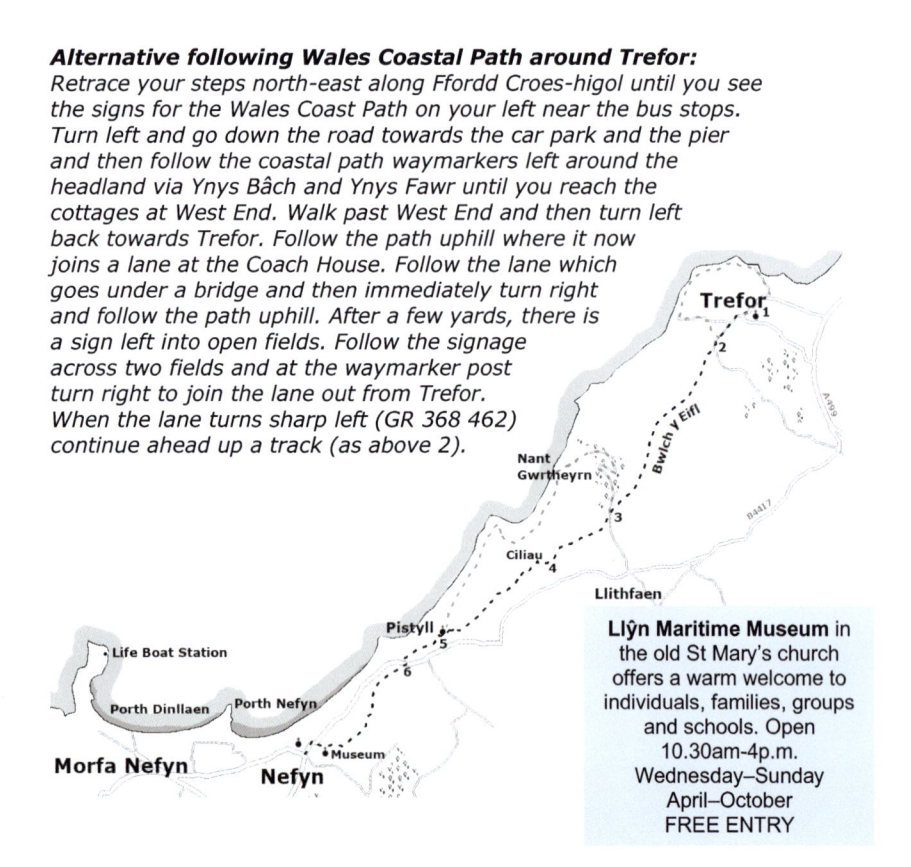

Alternative following Wales Coastal Path around Trefor:
Retrace your steps north-east along Ffordd Croes-higol until you see the signs for the Wales Coast Path on your left near the bus stops. Turn left and go down the road towards the car park and the pier and then follow the coastal path waymarkers left around the headland via Ynys Bâch and Ynys Fawr until you reach the cottages at West End. Walk past West End and then turn left back towards Trefor. Follow the path uphill where it now joins a lane at the Coach House. Follow the lane which goes under a bridge and then immediately turn right and follow the path uphill. After a few yards, there is a sign left into open fields. Follow the signage across two fields and at the waymarker post turn right to join the lane out from Trefor. When the lane turns sharp left (GR 368 462) continue ahead up a track (as above 2).

Llŷn Maritime Museum in the old St Mary's church offers a warm welcome to individuals, families, groups and schools. Open 10.30am–4p.m. Wednesday–Sunday April–October
FREE ENTRY

There are two possible routes from here to Pistyll.

The Inland Route:
3. 3.62km/2.3 miles (SH 353 439) From the car park walk towards Llysfaen and after a few metres walk diagonally right towards telegraph poles to go through a metal gate onto the bridle path. Keeping the ditch and fence on your right pass through another gate near the house (Tir Gwyn) on your left. Take the next gate to the right through the wall and walk up the middle of the field to the marker post which is visible on the brow of the hill. Pass through a field gate, seen ahead, turn half right following the earth mound on your right to join and follow a wall on your right and then turn right again through a small wooden gate. From here follow the path down towards the farm in the distance, ignoring a metal stile on your left.

4. 5.0km/3.1 miles (SH 342 432) Go over a stile onto a farm track, turn right and, in a few metres, take the footpath signed on the left. Follow this path crossing a stile and stay on it with the farm, Cilau Uchaf, on your right to reach the farm access track. Cross the track through two kissing gates and you now follow the waymarked path through several fields with metal kissing gates. After passing over the brow of a small hill you will see the bay of Porth Dinllaen in the distance which will be your guide as you now start to go down through more fields with kissing gates, passing by Cefneydd on your left. The path now leads you down past Ffynnon Sanctaidd to Pistyll and St. Beuno's Church.

The Coastal Path: *this winds its way down to The Welsh Language Centre (Nant Gwrtheyrn) and on towards the beach; from the ruined jetty climb a delightful but steep path to Ciliau-isaf (Farm) from there the path leads across the bwlch to St.Beuno's Church (at Pistyll) which comes into sight as you descend. This is waymarked as Wales Coast Path.)*

5. 7.02km/4.4 miles (SH328 422) After visiting the Church return to the lane and continue along it to pass the site of the new holiday development. You are now following the Wales Coast Path with new waymark posts as a guide.

6. 7.94km/5 miles (SH 321 418) On reaching the B4417 turn left and soon take the track on the right. The path crosses a couple of fields (quite muddy in wet times) but soon passes to the right of a house and then round the side of a hill, through the disused quarry workings to join an access track leading to a few houses. A narrow path soon forks right, near the end of which there is a small stream on your right. Where the path opens onto a public field bear right to go through a kissing gate onto a narrow path by the church wall. Turn left at St Mary's Church (now Llyn Maritime Museum), walk down the street to the main road and turn left into Nefyn.

Nefyn to Tudweiliog

14.5km / 9.0 miles
Total Ascent: 556m. **Total Descent:** 546m. Max. Elevation: 53m.
Refreshments: Nefyn, Towyn, Tudweiliog.
Toilets: Nefyn, Tudeiliog (pub)
Passport Stamps: Nefyn (Maritime Museum), Tudweiliog (Post Office)
OS Explorer Map 253

Along the coast path, stopping for refreshment at Ty Coch at Porth Dinllaen, skirting the golf course and looking out for seals and sea birds as you keep to the cliff top all the way to Towyn, where you can head inland to Tudweiliog.

1. 0.0km/ miles (SH 307 405) From the centre of Nefyn take the road Pen-y-Bryn (signed to Aberdaron). Pass St. David's Church on the right (Nanhoron Hotel on left). Take the 2nd road to the right - Lon Y Traeth; at the point where this road starts to descend steeply you can follow it and walk along the beach, alternatively bear left onto a signed footpath (Wales Coast Path / Pilgrim's Way). This follows the cliff top to Penrhyn Nefyn (seen ahead) and continues to Morfa Nefyn where you descend steps to the slipway to the beach.

There are two possible routes from here.

2. 3.25km/2 miles (SH 282 407) The longer and more challenging route takes you along the beach to Porth Dinllaen, past the lifeboat station to climb around the headland (very rough path) to the Golf Course. Here you can walk all the way around on the Wales Coast Path along the coastal edge to Abergeirch.

58

Shorter Route: Cross the road to the slipway and follow the Wales Coast Path up the steps, then go through the car park to the road and turn right and follow the road to the Golf Club. Go through the kissing gate to the right of the barrier and walk down the tarmac road (across the course) to the maintenance shed. Here a footpath sign guides you left across the hallowed turf then right to rejoin the Wales Coast Path which follows the edge of the Golf Course and at the end, the route plunges down to the inlet at Abergeirch.

3. 7.9km/4.9 miles (SH 267 404) The route now follows a magnificent coastal path for a good 5.6km/3.5 miles.

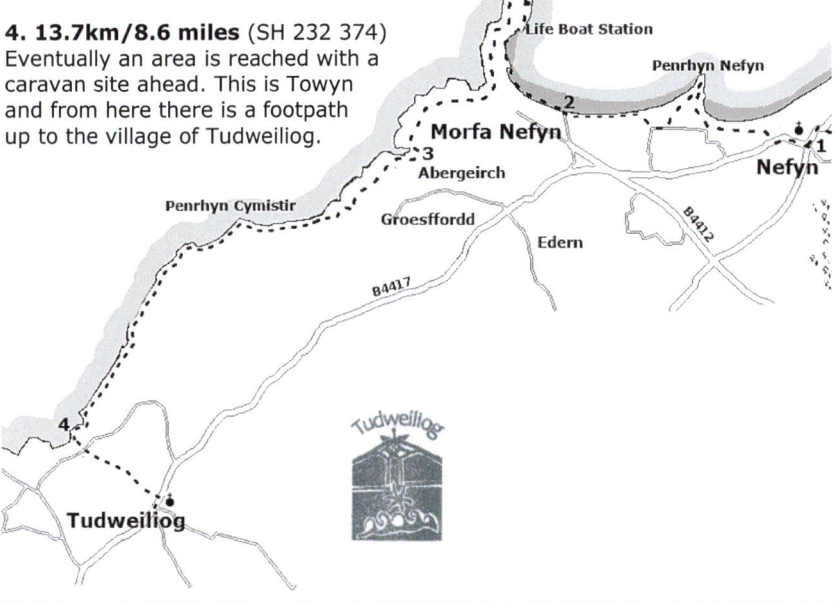

4. 13.7km/8.6 miles (SH 232 374) Eventually an area is reached with a caravan site ahead. This is Towyn and from here there is a footpath up to the village of Tudweiliog.

Tudweiliog to Aberdaron

19.8km / 12.4 miles
Total Ascent: 404m. **Total Descent:** 450m. Max. Elevation: 81.9m.
Refreshments: Tudweiliog, Towyn, Whistling Sands (Porthor), Aberdaron
Toilets: Tudweiliog (pub), Porthor (car park), Aberdaron.
Passport Stamps: Tudweiliog (shop), Aberdaron (church).
OS Explorer Map 253

Another day on the coast path as far as Porthor/Whistling Sands and a welcome café. Turning inland, following footpaths across farmland to eventually follow a little stream right into Aberdaron. An alternative route takes you via the Pilgrim Church at Llangwnadl.

1. 0.0km/ miles (SH 237 368) To access Towyn caravan site from Tudweiliog take the footpath just north of the Post Office across fields (muddy by gates) through the farmyard with the caravan site. Coffee, ice cream and snacks are available in season from the shop at the top of the path to the beach. From the caravan site continue following the Coast Path. The footpath sign directs you to the beach. *If you take this option, you will need to scramble up the cliff back to the path.* Alternatively, or if the tide is in, make for a bench overlooking the bay and follow the coast at a higher level. In places the path is no more than a sheep track along the top of low-lying cliffs. Take extra care above the inlet at Penrhyn Melyn where the path is undercut and in danger of crumbling. It could be slippery if wet. About half-way down Traeth Penllech, where the stream comes down to the sea, the path descends steeply. Care is required to go down, across the stream and up the other side. The path keeps to the coast via Porth Colmon and its car park. Continue along the Coast to a definite ravine and stream at Porth Widlin. *(There is now a route all the way to Porthor / Whistling Sands on the Wales Coast Path).*

2. 10.3km/6.4 miles (SH 183 323) When the Coast Path crosses the stream at Porth Widlin and goes directly ahead, turn left to follow the footpath to the lane. Turn right along the lane. Go ahead at the first T-junction then right and left at the next two.

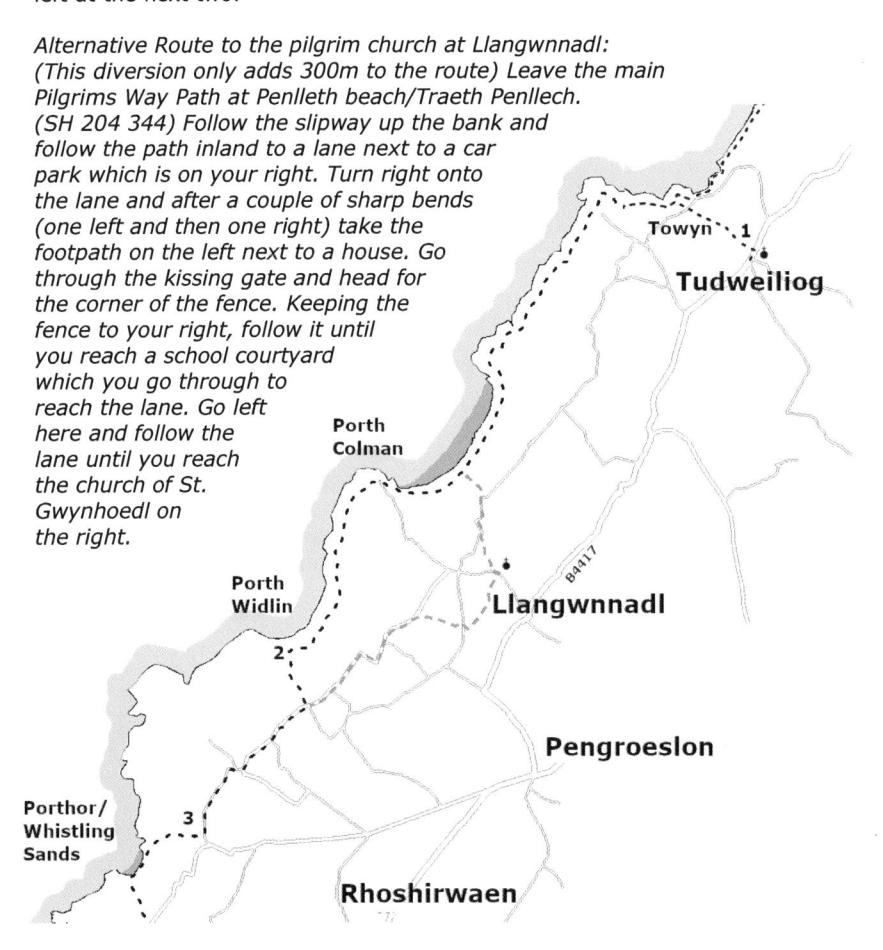

Alternative Route to the pilgrim church at Llangwnnadl:
(This diversion only adds 300m to the route) Leave the main Pilgrims Way Path at Penlleth beach/Traeth Penllech. (SH 204 344) Follow the slipway up the bank and follow the path inland to a lane next to a car park which is on your right. Turn right onto the lane and after a couple of sharp bends (one left and then one right) take the footpath on the left next to a house. Go through the kissing gate and head for the corner of the fence. Keeping the fence to your right, follow it until you reach a school courtyard which you go through to reach the lane. Go left here and follow the lane until you reach the church of St. Gwynhoedl on the right.

Leave the church and, turning right, go back along the lane. Look for a kissing gate on the left into a field and follow the hedge line until you reach another gate into a small dip. Turn half-left to go up the incline and across a field to another gate. Follow the fence to a farm and, going around to the right of it, join the farm lane to the road. Turn right onto the lane, and in about 50m turn left to go through a gate into a field and walk along the raised embankment. At the end of this raised feature you reach a field which you cross to a house. Go through the gate and, keeping the house on your left, find a gate in the top left-hand corner of the enclosure. This path is tightly enclosed by a hedge but follow this to the end and it brings you out to a lane where you continue left. Follow this lane to a junction where you take the right-hand fork. Stay on the lane until you pick up the Pilgrim's Way Path which comes in from your right from Porth Widlin a further 1500m down the lane. This then follows the North Wales Pilgrim's Way to Whistling Sands/Porthor.

3. 13.0km/8.1 miles (SH 173 303) After about 900 metres (and before the next road junction) take the footpath on the right which leads to the beach at Whistling Sands. Here there is a shop and cafe open during the season on the beach for a welcome cup of tea. Leaving the Wales Coast Path, walk up to the National Trust Car Park to the lane and turn right.

4. 15.0km/9.4 miles (SH 165 290)
In 40m at Carreg turn left along the track. Just before Tir-Bouog take the path on the right through three kissing gates. Then immediately turn left to go through a kissing gate on your left and then another through a wide hedge. Follow the path across two fields to the lane. Turn right.

The poet R. S. Thomas was vicar of St Hywyn's Church in Aberdaron from 1967 to 1978; when he retired he lived for some years in Y Rhiw. An ardent Welsh nationalist who learnt to speak Welsh, his poetry was based on his religious faith. In 1995 he was nominated for the Nobel Prize in Literature, and he was widely regarded as the best religious poet of his time.

The subject of one of Thomas's poems, Richard Robert Jones, better known as **"Dic Aberdaron"**, was born in the village in 1780. Despite very little formal education, he is said to have been fluent in 14 languages, and spent years travelling the country accompanied by his books and his cat. His grave is in St Asaph at the Parish Church.

62

5. 16.9km/10.6 miles (SH 175 282) Just past the crossroads take the footpath on the left and follow this towards Hendre Uchaf. Crossing the field, keep to the left-hand side going through two gates. Cross the middle of the next two fields, through kissing gates. Follow the path towards a large barn, taking the farm track to the right of the farm between the farm and the barn. Follow the farm road to the B4413.

6. 17.9km/11.1 miles (SH 179 274) Cross over to the track opposite. After about 400 metres, at a gate signed Cefn Coch, the path leaves the track over a stile on the right. The path keeps to the right of the hedge until you come to a wind affected hawthorn with a signpost behind it. Follow the path through the bushes. At the bottom of the hill go right towards a footbridge and turn right in front of it. You now follow the path with the river on your left until it eventually climbs right around a landslip. Go through the gate and stay to the right of the fence. This leads into Aberdaron.

You can pick up a Pilgrimage Completion Certificate at the National Trust Centre Porth y Swnt in Aberdaron.

From Aberdaron to Porth Meudwy, 1.8km / 1.2 miles (or 2.7km/1.7 miles by road): The ferry for Ynys Enlli (Bardsey Island) leaves from Porth Meudwy. To walk there take the road up the hill at the bridge signed Porth Meudwy and Mynydd Mawr and then follow the Wales Coast Path where it branches to the left and keeps to the top of the cliff. Follow it to Porth Meudwy.

You must book the ferry in advance on 07971 769 895. There is a café on the island that offers hot drinks and snacks. You can also visit the Bird Observatory and shop and an exhibition in the old schoolhouse.

Alternative route from Porthor to Aberdaron: 11.8km/7.4 miles along the Wales Coast Path.
The Coast Path provides several opportunities for variation. It can be followed all the way around the coast. This walk is similar to the path that you have followed from Nefyn. The advantage of this is that you should be able to see Ynys Enlli/ Bardsey Island even if you cannot visit. Alternatively, you can leave anywhere along the coast and take the lanes direct to Aberdaron.

Passport Stamps

Passport Stamps

Passport Stamps

Passport Stamps

Printed in Great Britain
by Amazon